Miracles II:
"Greater Miracles"

By
R.W. Schambach

All Scripture quotations are from the *King James Version* of the Bible.

Miracles II: "Greater Miracles"
ISBN 1-888361-52-2
Copyright © 2003 by R.W. Schambach
P.O. Box 9009
Tyler, Texas 75711

Contents

FINANCIAL MIRACLES

MIRACLES ON FOREIGN SOIL

Preface
"GREATER MIRACLES"

I believe in miracles!

If you cut all the miracles out of the Bible, you would not have a Bible left. It's a book of the miraculous, because our God is a miracle-working God. And my Bible declares that He is the same yesterday, today and forever! You know what that means? It means He is still doing today what He did yesterday. He's still doing the miraculous! In fact, I believe we are going to see greater miracles in this last day than we have ever seen before.

Some folks don't believe this. They say the days of miracles are over. You can even hear this from the pulpit. Some preachers say that the miraculous was only for the early church. But God has not changed. He is still in the miracle business.

The power of God is real today just like it was two thousand years ago. I've seen hundreds of miracles with my own eyes - people being healed and set free by the power of the living Christ!

I get so many letters, phone calls, and e-mails from people who have received miracles from God. In my meetings, people come back to testify of how the Lord touched their lives. It blesses my heart to hear these stories of what God has done. I like to share them with the world, to let people know that God is not dead, but He is alive, and He's doing great things in all the earth. That is the reason for this book - to let the world know what the Lord has done.

Some years ago I put out a book entitled *Miracles: Eyewitness to the Miraculous*. It catalogued some of the greatest miracles that I had seen and heard throughout my years of ministry. But it's not over. Hallelujah! God is still doing what He does best. *"Miracles ll"* is a book filled with more stories of people who received a special touch from God. I want you to hear their stories.

What do you have need of? You can pinpoint it. Maybe you need a healing in your body. Maybe your back is against the wall financially. Maybe you have a son who is hooked on drugs, bound by the devil, or a daughter who has run away from home. I don't care what the need is; God will perform a miracle in your life.

Your family may say you are crazy for believing God for a miracle. Your friends may look at you funny. Even your preacher may tell you that God doesn't work miracles anymore. Just let them talk. Let every man and let every devil be a liar, but let God be true! If He said it, He will do it! And if He spoke it, He will bring it to pass. No ifs, ands, buts or maybes.

"If you abide in Me, and My words abide in you, you will ask what you desire, and it shall be done for you. By this My Father is glorified, that you bear much fruit; so you will be My disciples...You did not choose Me, but I chose you and appointed you that you should go and bear fruit, and that your fruit should remain, that whatever you ask the Father in My name He may give you." (John 15:7-8,16)

Do you believe it? I'm telling you, folks, God's power works! If it didn't work, I would not have been in this for so long. I'd have done something else. But I cannot deny the power of God at work in the lives of people today – and when you hear these stories, you won't be able to either.

So as you read this book, let faith come alive in your heart. Just like these people, you will be a recipient of the "greater miracles" that God is doing in this last day.

MIRACLES OF SALVATION AND DELIVERANCE

FOREWORD

Do you believe in miracles? Oh, I know that most of you, my old time Partners do, but believe me, there are multitudes out there — EVEN IN SOME CHURCHES — who do not!

Well, the skeptics have reached most of us too late! We have seen with our own eyes the impossible, awesome miracles of our God!

One man who has seen more than most is R.W. Schambach. Wow! Wait till you read not one — but TWO — of his books describing his personal encounters with God's miracles!

How about, *"Forty Tumors and a Handkerchief"*! *"I Died Last Night"*! *"Spit in My Eyes"*! *"Fortuneteller's Nightmare"*! *"Man Spared from Electric Chair"*! And one of my favorites: *"What Mohammed Couldn't Do"*!

You know, in a court of law, the "EYE WITNESS" wins the case! Well, believe me, every case here is WON because we have many "eyewitnesses"!

Use these books to confound the skeptics and bring many to healing and to faith in Jesus Christ!

> Paul F. Crouch
> President
> Trinity Broadcasting Network

INTRODUCTION
"THE GREATEST MIRACLE"

Praise God! I never get tired of talking about miracles. I have seen so many amazing miracles throughout my years of preaching the gospel. But still, the greatest miracle by far is when God reaches down, takes out a stony heart and puts in a heart of flesh - when He takes a filthy sinner, clothes him with the righteousness of God, and writes his name in the Lamb's Book of Life. There is no greater miracle.

This is what God wants to do for every person on the face of the earth. When He revealed His promised deliverer, Jesus Christ, He provided a way for everyone to receive this miracle.

In the city of Nazareth, at the beginning of Jesus' early ministry, He stood up in the temple one day to read a very significant scripture that revealed His heart for ministry and outlined the earthly mission His Father had given Him:

"The Spirit of the Lord is upon Me, Because He has anointed Me To preach the gospel to the poor; He has sent Me to heal the brokenhearted, To proclaim liberty to the captives And recovery of sight to the blind, To set at liberty those who are oppressed; To proclaim the acceptable year of the Lord." (Luke 4:18-19)

Jesus was quoting from the book of Isaiah. As He read, a synagogue filled with religious people noticed something different about this young rabbi. The words were not simply being recited; they were being adopted as a personal creed. Jesus was revealing Himself as the fulfillment of this specific prophecy.

Now anyone enslaved by sin, oppressed by the devil, owned by corruption and evil, could make a clean break from their old lives and start over by accepting Jesus Christ as Deliverer and Savior. No matter how much of a sinner a person may be, God has a great miracle of deliverance waiting for them.

In the next pages you will read some outstanding testimonies of deliverance I have witnessed. Just remember, when Christ comes into the heart of an individual, when all things become new, that person has received the greatest miracle!

1
PRIZEFIGHTER GOES DOWN FOR THE COUNT

When I was pastoring in Newark, New Jersey, there was a dear woman in our church named Sister Price. She came to me one night about her husband. He was an old "boozer." All he did was drink. No matter how hard she tried, she could never get him to come to church with her.

She said, "Brother Schambach, you don't know what kind of devil I married. I've done everything for him, but he won't come to church with me. I've tried everything. I'm tired of it!"

"Well, I'm glad you're tired of it," I told her.

"You mean I can leave him?"

"Oh no, girl," I said. "You picked him out all by yourself. You said you're tired of it? Good. Now we're going to put it in God's hands."

So I laid hands on her and said, "Holy Ghost, sic him! Knock him down and drag him to the foot of the cross!"

I was running a revival there in Newark so we had a service the next night. During the meeting, this big guy came in. He was about six foot two, two hundred and seventy pounds. Solid steel! And he came walking up that center aisle like he owned the place.

I jumped off that platform and headed down toward him. I was walking like I owned the place. I met him face to face, head-on, jaw to jaw – an irresistible force meeting an immovable object.

"Are you the preacher?"

"Yes, sir," I said. "I'm the man of God here."

"They tell me you can help me."

"You smell like you need help, brother."

Then he said sarcastically, "You want to help me? Buy me a fifth of liquor!"

I felt my fist doubling up. The old Schambach was coming alive, the one that's supposed to be crucified with Christ. Do you know what I'm talking about? I wanted to give him a knuckle sandwich right there! But my hand went limp. The Holy Ghost wouldn't allow me to hit him. And boy, am I glad! I found out later that he was an all-state boxing champ!

So I went to lay hands on him, but the Holy Ghost wouldn't even let me touch him. I got about two inches from him and he just fell back - BAM! He hit solid concrete!

Then Sister Price ran out shouting, "Aaahh! Glory! That's that devil I'm married to!" (How come all these women are married to the same husband?)

I said, "Hush, woman. Don't say anymore. He's here now. Let the Holy Ghost do His job now." So he lay there on that floor.

When he got up he was sober, and ready to receive Christ as his Savior. God saved him, and filled him with the Holy Ghost and fire. He was speaking in other tongues and praising God!

God worked a miracle! He made a lamb out of a lion. After that, Brother Price preached the gospel for many years in New York, New Jersey, Virginia, North Carolina and all over the East Coast. He has gone home to be with the Lord, but his wife, dear Sister Price, is still singing and telling the story of how God made her violent old husband a new creature through the delivering power of Jesus Christ.

2
FROM JUNK TO JESUS

I have many friends who have helped partner with my ministry over the years. A lot of them have great stories of what God has done for them through my ministry. I'll never forget the story of a certain partner of mine, Brother James Wallace, another "lost cause" who was transformed by the power of Christ.

In August of 1975 I had my tent up in the Bronx, New York. Many preachers are afraid to go into the ghetto - into places like the Bronx. But I love to take the gospel where it is needed! I love to take it right into the heart of the inner city; to see God perform miracles and deliver those that are bound by the devil. You see, a lot of these folks won't set foot in a church. So I bring church to them. People who wouldn't go into a church come pouring into my tent meetings, and that's when God takes over!

Now, James Wallace was just that kind of person. He was raised in one of the most hellish neighborhoods of the Bronx. At an early age he had experimented with many different types of pills and drugs, and as a teenager became an alcoholic.

Circumstances from his environment and his own young rebellion filled him with a violent rage. He broke the law often and found himself in and out of police precincts and jail. James adopted the attitudes of his environment — he trusted no one but himself. Eventually he became a racist, hating all white people.

In his early twenties, James was living with his girlfriend, not wanting to marry her because he knew he would be a high-risk father in many ways. Life went from bad to worse when the doctors told him he had cirrhosis of the liver. James needed help.

In the eyes of man, he was not a likely candidate for salvation. But what is impossible with man is possible with God!

One day James pulled up in his car to 149th Street and the Major Deegan Expressway in the Bronx. He was parked in front of a Gospel tent that was as big as a football field. It looked like a circus tent. All he could hear was the voice of a preacher who was shouting about something.

James felt that anger rising up within him. The preacher was a white man, and as far as he could tell, he was preaching about a white God named Jesus. Against his better judgment, James went inside to see what was happening.

The preacher, R.W. Schambach, was telling people that Jesus could free them from sin, heal their bodies and deliver them from addictions.

Then, he asked some people from the vast audience to come forward and tell others what Jesus had done for them. James heard stories of deaf ears opening, drug addicts being instantly set free and people being healed from cancer. One thread of every story was the same — each of the storytellers said Jesus had done the work in their lives. At first, James refused to believe what he was hearing. He thought all preachers were either pimps or sissies. Yet, James could not deny there was something powerful and real happening under that tent.

Night after night he would come back to listen. Then one night James mustered up the courage to go forward and let the preacher pray for him.

When the preacher prayed for him, James said a prayer, "God, if you're real, let me feel something."

James didn't feel anything right away. In his mind he was saying, "See, I knew this thing was fake. Nothing happened."

He went right across the street to the bar and ordered some drinks.

But that night he realized something. He had lost his taste and needs for alcohol. He had no more shakes. He had no withdrawal symptoms. He was free from alcohol, and he knew it.

The next night, James went back to the tent. He knelt at an altar and asked Jesus Christ to forgive him. When James got off his knees, he was delivered from his addictions and healed of cirrhosis of the liver. Today, he is married, has four children and is pastoring a church in the Bronx.

James is still partnering with my ministry today. He serves as a testimony of the power of God to set the captives free! In his own words:

"Jesus is the answer. He set me free from pushing dope to preaching hope. From crime to Christ. From junk to Jesus."

3
BROKEN NEEDLES AND A PHONE CALL

You can stand in faith for a loved one, believing that God will save them and deliver them. This is what I call 'proxy.' When two or more are uniting their faith in perfect agreement, God will perform a miracle. I want to share two stories with you about people who stood proxy for their loved ones.

Back in the 1960's I rented a synagogue in Philadelphia, and I held a revival there for two weeks. While I was there, an elderly woman came to see me about her son, who was hooked on drugs. She said, "He has come into the house and stolen every light. He stole the couch. He stole the rugs. My house is bare! He took it all and sold it to pump into his arm!"

When you're hooked on drugs, you're going to find it somewhere. Every one of you that used to be a drug addict (or still are one) knows what I'm talking about. You'll find it somewhere.

She said, "I can't get him to church."

"He doesn't have to come to church," I told her. Then I laid hands on her and prayed the same prayer that I prayed for Brother Price in Newark. "Holy Ghost, get him!"

After I prayed, the Lord gave me a prophetic word for the woman. "Go on home. Your son is delivered."

You might say, 'Well, anyone could have said that to her.' But I was operating under the anointing of the Holy Ghost. He doesn't lie! So I knew that her son was delivered.

I came back to the synagogue the next night. The same little lady had come back to the service. This time she had a young man with her. She got my attention. This young man had a story to tell. There's always a story to tell. Hallelujah!

The night before he had been in an alley with a needle, trying to give himself a shot when the needle broke. But, drug addicts are used to that. They always carry a spare in their billfold. So he pulled the spare out and tried to inject it into his arm. Then that needle broke!

He had to have a quick fix, so he went to his pusher's apartment. (Now, from what I'm told, that's a no-no!)

He beat on the door. The guy opened the door.

"What are you doing at my house?" he said. "Get in here!"

"Man, I need a quick fix," the young man told him. "I got the drugs from you earlier, but I broke two needles. Get me a needle, I need a shot now."

So the pusher went to get him another needle.

What this young man told me next thrilled me. Right there in the pusher's apartment, something left him. He suddenly had no cravings for the drug. Right there in front of the pusher, a miracle took place!

The pusher tried to force it on him. "Here's the needle. Give yourself ---"

"No wait. I don't need it. Something happened, I don't know what it was."

Then he gave the drugs back that he had bought earlier. Now, this is another no-no to the drug addict. But he was delivered! He was set free! He didn't need them anymore.

That night, his mama was coming home from church. If you've ever been to our meetings, you know we keep them a little lengthy. She was getting back to her house around midnight. To her surprise, her son showed up. This was early for him. He never came in before two, three, or four o'clock in the morning. (It didn't matter. He didn't have a bed anyway. He had stolen it and sold it already.)

When his mama saw him coming up those steps she said, "What are you doing home so early?"

He said, "Mother, I don't know. Something happened to me tonight." And he told her the story I told you.

"Oh!" she said. "Brother Schambach laid hands on me and sent the Word to you and commanded that devil to turn you loose. That monkey is off of your back right now!"

Oh, hallelujah! He was in the service that night and got saved, sanctified and filled with the Holy Ghost.

There was another lady who came to me one time. She said, "Oh, Brother Schambach. I have a daughter that ran away from home, and I don't know where she is. I haven't heard from her for 6 years."

And I said, "God will do it." Then I prayed that same prayer. "Holy Ghost, get her! Knock her down where she is! Bring her to the foot of the cross. And tonight, make her dial her mother's phone number."

When I got done, I looked at that woman and said, "Go home and sit by the phone. You're going to get a call from your daughter."

She came back the next night shouting and jumping. She had a great testimony. She said, "Brother Schambach, it was just like you said. When I got home, I sat by the phone. My daughter called me for the first time in six years. She said, 'I don't know why I'm calling you, but something got a hold of me.' I said, 'That's the Holy Ghost!'"

This is proxy! You can believe for somebody else. God knows what to do. If He can find two of us here on earth agreeing, as touching anything that they shall ask, it shall be done.

Are you ready to see that loved one set free? Well, you're going to put your faith to work. You're going to stand proxy for them, and God's going to give you the miracle that you've been praying for. Let's pray, shall we?

Father, in the name of Jesus, we ask that You touch the life of this lost loved one right now. Put a hook in their jaw and drag them to the foot of Calvary. Arrest them in their tracks. Get a hold of them, in Jesus' name. Save them and fill them with the Holy Ghost. We thank You for Your miracle-working power. We ask this in the name of Jesus. Amen and amen.

4
THE VOICE OF POWER

I love ministering to people through radio broadcasts. I've been on radio for many years now. There's just something about it. You see, when people hear a broadcast, they can't sit back and judge the preacher because of the way he looks or acts. They can't sit back and say, "Well, I don't like his tie. I don't like his suit. I don't like him!"

They can only judge a preacher by what he says. So when I preach on radio, people can only judge me by the Word of God that I bring forth, not by how I dress or what color I am. In fact, many people think I'm a black preacher!

God has saved and delivered so many people through the "Voice of Power" broadcast (now called "Power Today"). I have three testimonies that I want to share of people that were at the end of their ropes — at the point of suicide — when they heard an old fashioned Holy Ghost preacher on their radio. God delivered them.

There was a gentleman in Boston who seemed like he had it all. He was a successful businessman. He had a new house, a new car, and a fine family. But he had one downfall — he was an alcoholic.

This tore his life apart. It cost him his job and eventually his family left him.

"I couldn't afford milk for my baby," he later testified, "But I still bought the booze."

He soon lost his house, too. The last day he was there, he sat alone in that empty house (the furniture was already gone). He figured that he might as well end it all there. He planned to commit suicide.

He turned up the radio as loud as it would go so his neighbors wouldn't hear the gun go off when he shot himself.

Just as he was about to pull the trigger, he heard a voice on the radio. It was the voice of a loud, Pentecostal preacher who singled him out.

"Don't touch that dial! Suicide is not your answer! Put your hand on the radio right now, and I'll pray for that spirit of oppression and suicide to leave you."

Immediately, he went to his radio, cradled it in his arms, and prayed that prayer with me. Right there in that empty house, he gave his life to Christ and was instantly delivered from alcoholism.

He got his family back, and found an even better job than the one he had lost. In just two years, he was able to pay for a new home as well.

Another man that God delivered through radio was a brother named Montgomery, who had been a pastor. After his church split, he had left the ministry and went into construction.

His church wasn't the only thing that split. He and his wife went through a divorce. His life was falling apart piece by piece.

One morning, a spirit of oppression swept over him, urging him to commit suicide. He tried to stand up against it, but nothing worked. He wanted to kill himself.

That night, he fell into bed and cried out, "God, I put myself in Your care."

God answered him, "Son, I'm sending a prophet." Of course, John had no idea what that meant. At 3:00 in the morning, he turned on the radio in desperation. The "Voice of Power" broadcast was on. At the end of the message, he heard the same kind of charge that the man from Boston had heard.

"Don't turn your radio off. I'm going to pray for someone very specifically...that young preacher who has been tormented by a spirit of suicide today. You foul spirit, I curse you in the name of the Lord Jesus." As soon as I spoke those words, the oppression left instantly and never returned.

The final story is one that came across my desk many years ago from Canada.

There was a family of two parents and three daughters. They were facing a crisis time financially; no one in the household was able to find a job to meet their needs. They literally could not put food on the table.

A heavy depression settled in on the father and spread to the entire family. He and his wife decided it would be better if they all died together, right now, instead of waiting for starvation. So the family formed a suicide pact. They planned to end it all in their garage, inhaling the carbon monoxide fumes.

When the day arrived, they took their places in the car. The father started the car up, but then the mother reached across and shut off the ignition.

"What if we wait just one more day?" she pleaded.

Angrily, the father jumped out of the car. If his wife persisted, he would lose his nerve. He hoped he would be able to get back in the car tomorrow.

In his anger, he went in the house and started kicking things around. Finally, he turned on the radio. The radio man was new to him, but what the preacher was saying captured his attention. The preacher was talking about a demon of suicide that convinces people there's no hope. "Mister, suicide is not the answer to your problems. Jesus Christ is the only answer."

This was the first time the father had heard about Jesus, who not only could save a life from sin, but was able to deliver from all kinds of oppression, including thoughts of suicide.

The entire family realized that tormenting spirit was trying to destroy their lives and send them to hell. On their knees in the living room, an entire family repented of their sins and received Jesus as Lord of their home. Within days, God turned their situation around.

5
WHAT A LOVELY BRIDE

In 1991, I conducted a crusade at a church in Tyler, Texas. This is the area where my ministry headquarters are located in East Texas. Now, this crusade was not in a tent lot. It was not in the inner city. It was in a church. But the devil still showed up. Ol' Slewfoot was looking for a fight. Well, he was messing with the wrong preacher!

Several months before the meeting, a call had come to Rose Heights from a young lady who desperately needed help. She had been involved in the occult, and was now under the control of demonic spirits.

"The Joshua Team," a group of believers in that church dedicated to praying and interceding for such cases, went into action. As she struggled to get free of the devil's hold on her, this group prayed continually for her deliverance.

She tried to get to church, but these oppressive spirits kept her from entering. She would sometimes drive into the church parking lot, only to drive away under their power. She even tried to enter the church, but then left again. There was a battle raging on for her soul.

The devil told her she would die on October 31st (Halloween), and become his bride. When that date passed and she was still alive, she began to have hope. After receiving counseling, she was convinced that God loved her.

On the Sunday before the crusade, she saw an ad about the meetings, and made up her mind to come. And this time she made it. God was getting ready to move. The devil didn't stand a chance!

At 10:30 that Saturday night, November 23, "Joshua Team" members led her down the aisle for prayer. But the devil doesn't give up without a fight. You can imagine what he must have been telling her as she walked toward the platform.

I laid hands on her, and there was an intense spiritual struggle. But it didn't last long. The demonic forces had to go, because the devil is no match for the power of God, and my Bible says greater is He that is in me (and greater is He that is in you!) than he that is in the world! (I John 4:4)

As the spirits that controlled her left her body, she renounced the devil and received Christ. Glory to God! That night she had her first good night's sleep in a long, long time. For the first time in her life, she was free. The devil had told her she would be his bride, but now she is the Bride of Christ!

In **Mark 16:17**, Jesus says, **"And these signs will follow those that believe: In my name they will cast out demons."** Hallelujah!

Most of the church today is running from devils. I hear so many of these prayer requests. "Pray for me, the devil's after me." Well stop running! Turn around and run after him. My God, send HIM to the prayer line! Let him know that some believers are on his trail. One of you shall chase a thousand, and two of you shall put ten thousand to flight!

"Behold, I give you the authority to trample on serpents and scorpions, and over all the power of the enemy, and nothing shall by any means hurt you." **(Luke 10:19)**

Beloved, we've got more power than the devil!

6
ANOINTING OIL ENDS DEMONIC NIGHTMARE

God works miracles in many different ways. He uses many different vehicles to display His power in the lives of people. After all, He is a creative God.

One of these is anointing oil. The Bible teaches that oil is to be used to anoint for needs in the name of our Lord (see *James 5:14*). Now, the oil has no special power in itself, but God often works miracles through its use by the believer. I have seen this many times.

I have anointed many people and have seen God do miraculous things because of it. Then sometimes I distribute oil to other believers so that they can anoint others. I send out many bottles of oil absolutely free to those who request it for needs in their life.

I had a woman and her husband write to my ministry once, requesting the anointing oil for Rosemary, the woman's mother.

For seven months, Rosemary had been demon-possessed. She couldn't eat or drink. Under the evil influence, she broke all the windows in her house and rolled around on the floor. Three grown men could not hold her down! The demons inside her would howl, and the coyotes outside would answer their call.

She was placed in a mental institution, where she stayed for six months. All that time, her daughter and son-in-law prayed for her. Day and night they prayed. It was during this time that they had written to me requesting the oil. They anointed Rosemary and prayed for her deliverance.

Well, some time later, Rosemary herself came back to one of my meetings to testify. She was free! She told the story of how her daughter had anointed her and prayed for her. She was delivered by the power of God! She steadily began to get better, and her physical body was restored as well.

This blesses me! Jesus Christ is still at work today, setting the captives free just like he was two thousand years ago. He's just looking for people that know how to believe His Word and stand on His promises. When we are obedient to His voice, He can work miracles through us.

7
SECOND CHANCE

In my meetings, before I preach, I like to have people come to the platform and testify about what God has done in their lives. I love doing this because when people in the audience hear these powerful testimonies, faith begins to stir in their hearts, and then they are ready to receive their own miracle from God.

One night, while I had my tent up in Coney Island, New York, a woman named Lucy came up to the platform with a story to tell.

When she was thirteen years of age, she became a lesbian. She started dressing like a man and acting like a man. The devil even had her believing that she was a man! Soon she began using drugs. She hated this lifestyle, but she could not break free. Everything seemed hopeless. She even tried to commit suicide twice. But she failed at that, too.

After twenty-four years of this torture, she developed herpes.

Once again, in man's eyes, there was no hope for Lucy. It seemed like the end - like it was too late for anything to help her. But it's never too late for Jesus! Hallelujah! He's always right on time!

Maybe your situation seems hopeless. Maybe everybody else has given up on you. I don't care whether you're a drug addict, a homosexual, a lesbian, or on your deathbed with some type of infirmity, Jesus Christ is your cure. It's never too late for Him to perform a miracle!

But back to Lucy. Here she was, sick and dying in her sin. She stood in her bathroom, shaking and scared to death. She didn't want to die. She knew she would go to hell. But in this moment of desperation, she heard a voice. It was the voice of God!

"This is your last chance I am giving you," the voice said to her.

So there in the bathroom, Lucy cried out to God. "Lord, I just want to serve You. Change me because I don't want to be like this anymore!"

Instantly, she was free. Every bit of demonic oppression left her. The sickness departed from her body. God restored her mind, and her womanhood. He saved her and set her feet on the right path. When she told us the story under the tent, she was feeling great.

That's the kind of God I serve! He gives us a second chance. If He didn't, this old preacher would have been dead a long time ago. But I'm so glad that He's in the business of restoring people who seem hopeless to everybody else.

8
REBEL WITH A PRAYING MAMA

There is another individual who likes to come into my meetings and testify about how God delivered him. Doc is his name, and he's a pastor in Gloucester City, New Jersey. Now, he's not your ordinary pastor. He's got tattoos all over and drives a motorcycle. But he loves Jesus and he loves to see souls brought into the Kingdom of God. He's a perfect example of how God answers prayer.

Now, Doc hasn't always lived for the Lord. He spent thirty years as a criminal in a motorcycle gang. He was bound by drugs and alcohol. He was depressed and mentally disturbed. He was in and out of jail for the crimes he committed. Not exactly pastor material, in the world's eyes.

But he had a praying mama! All those thirty years she prayed for God to turn his life around. She would often come to visit him in prison. She would tell him about Jesus.

"Oh, if you only knew Jesus," she would say.

"Mom, I'm too far gone," he told her. "Jesus won't have anything to do with me."

Well you know what? Jesus has something to do with everybody!

His mama never stopped praying. Then one night in 1987, Doc ended up in the service of a little Assemblies of God church. But he wasn't ready to get saved yet.

So he went up in front of the pastor (who was a much smaller man than he) and started screaming at him all the things that he had done wrong in his life. See, he wanted to get out of there, and he thought the pastor would throw him out after all that. But the pastor just looked at him and said, "Doc, Jesus loves you just the way you are. If you will let Him, He'll change you."

Something happened inside of Doc that he couldn't explain. All those years of praying that his mama had put into him paid off. God got a hold of that man, saved him, and turned his life around completely.

Now he's pastoring a church in Gloucester City, right in the middle of all the drug addicts, pushers and prostitutes. Some people told him he was too old to start a church. But if you will remember, Moses was 80 before God used him. Doc is still a boy!

He's doing great things for the Lord now. I remember at one of my tent meetings, Doc brought a guy to me who had been doing a bag of dope outside the tent. We prayed for the young man and God delivered him. Now he is clean and sober, and is a member of Doc's church. Hallelujah! God sets you free so you can set somebody else free!

So all of you praying mothers out there, don't give up on your sons. Don't give up on your daughters. Just keep on keeping on! It ain't over 'til it's over. God's going to save your entire household, and you are going to be able to come back and give God praise for what He has done.

9
MODERN-DAY JONAH

When I was preaching in Canada one year, I had another brother come up to the platform to testify - Pastor Paul. I tell you folks, I was so glad to hear his story because sometimes as preacher you wonder, 'Is anybody listening out there?' Just to hear a testimony like his makes me want to shout. Let me tell you what happened.

This young man was a former drug dealer in Winnipeg. He had been hooked on crack and all sorts of other drugs. He would go out on binges and get stoned out of his mind. He did all this because he was running from God.

You see, at the age of three, God had called Paul to preach. Although he remembered that very clearly, he continued to run from the call on his life. He didn't want to have anything to do with God.

Yet, he could not get away from the conviction of the Holy Spirit, Who kept telling him God had something better for him.

So he tried to drown out that voice with drugs.

He ended up bed-ridden in his parents' basement for three months. He was miserable, and didn't want to live anymore. So in that basement, he cried out, "God, if You're real, come into my life. If not, I'll just kill myself! I have nothing to live for!"

Instantly, God took away his craving for drugs. Oh, I love this — instantly! Listen to me, if God could save this young man, he can save anybody!

God was not done with him yet. After all, He'd called him to preach. When God calls you to do something, He means business!

So in that basement of his parents' house, Paul started reading the Bible from cover to cover. He was so hungry for more of God that he started digging through boxes there in the basement, where he found three sermon LP's by an old-fashioned Holy Ghost preacher named Schambach. These sermons had been spiritual food for his parents when they were seeking the Lord.

He listened to them over and over again. They gave him a foundation in his knowledge of God's Word. He heard about healing the sick, casting out devils, and bringing lost souls to Christ.

Now Paul is a pastor in North Carolina, and has his own miracle ministry. He told me that people are being healed of polio, healed of cancer, and that cataracts are disappearing! He has been to nine countries, preaching the gospel of Christ, and has led hundreds to the Lord.

He came all the way from North Carolina to one of my meetings up in Canada just to shake my hand and let me know what the Lord had done. Hallelujah!

I'll tell you, when God calls somebody, he knows what He's doing! He knows the work that He has in mind for them to accomplish. I'm so glad that my sermons were able to help this man grow in his walk with the Lord.

You know, those same old sermons that I used to preach, the ones he heard in the basement, I'm still preaching them today! Some people get on to me about that. They say, "Brother Schambach, you're still preaching the same thing that you did twenty years ago."

You know what I tell them? I say, "Thank you. You just paid me the greatest compliment!"

God's Word does not change! Hallelujah! I'm not changing my message for anybody! I'm going to keep preaching that same gospel of power until the Lord takes me home.

10
WALKING THE STREETS OF SOUTH PHILADELPHIA

The Bible says, *"God has not given us a spirit of fear"* (*2 Timothy 1:7*). It also says, *"fear involves torment"* (*1 John 4:18*). Therefore, I can conclude that fear is a tormenting spirit. Many of God's people are bound by this tormenting spirit of fear, even when they hear the Word preached.

Fear is the opposite of faith. It can keep you from being active as a Christian. If you are bound with a spirit of fear, I don't have to tell you — you need a miracle of deliverance. And I have good news — God wants you to be rid of fear in your life, and is ready and willing to set you free.

Once, when I was in Philadelphia, I met a woman who had a problem with fear.

I used to conduct private interviews, where people could come and meet with me one on one. This lady came in trying to make an impression. She talked in tongues a little and then sat down.

I said, "What can I do for you?"

She said, "I've come for you to pray for me."

I said, "I don't pray in the daytime. I pray at night. You see, we preach in the daytime to stir your faith. Then we lay hands on you during the night service when that faith is alive."

She said, "Well, I can't come at night."

I said, "Are you working?"

"No."

"Do you have an appointment?"

"No."

"Then come back tonight," I told her.

"I'm not coming back."

I said, "Well, I'm not praying."

That might seem harsh, but I knew she was hiding something from me. I discerned it in my own spirit. So I asked her, "What's your problem? I want to know."

She said, "Well, I've got high blood pressure, and I've got sugar diabetes."

"Is that all?" I said.

"Yes, it is," she replied.

I said, "No, you're telling me a lie. You're telling me you can't come tonight. The reason why you can't come is because you're bound with a spirit of fear."

She said, "How did you know?"

Listen, she was a child of God. She loved the Lord. But she was still bound by that spirit of fear.

She said, "I haven't been out of my house at night for the last 12 years. Oh, Brother Schambach, this spirit torments me."

I said, "Look, stay until tonight. Go next door and buy a sandwich. Stay here and I'll pray for you tonight. I'll get rid of that spirit of fear. God's given me the power to cast out devils, and I'm going to liberate you from that foul spirit that's tormenting your mind. If you stay, and God doesn't deliver you, my wife and I will personally take you home."

She said, "You'll do that?"

I said, "I'll do it. I'll even go into your house first. You can stay with my wife in the car. I'll turn on every light, look behind the couch and the chairs, open your closet, and make sure there's nobody around there."

She was convinced. She said, "Well, if you'll do that I'll stay."

After I preached that night, I called her up first for prayer. I laid hands on her and the power of God hit her and knocked her flat on her back. I laid hands on about 500 people that night.

After it was all over, my wife and I were looking for the woman because I'd promised to give her a ride home. But I couldn't find her anywhere! I ran outside and looked all over the place. I said, "Oh, Lord. I've got to find that woman." I never did.

The next night she came back into the meeting shouting and rejoicing. At night!

I said, "Come on up here. I know you've got a testimony."

She told the people the story I told you. She said, "I know Brother Schambach told me he and his wife would take me home last night. But I didn't have to let them take me home because when he laid hands on me, that devil of fear left. God delivered me and set me free! I walked the whole way home."

I said, "You walked? In Philadelphia!"

Now I was getting nervous! She lived 30 blocks away in South Philadelphia. That meant she had walked through the worst part of town! This was the same woman that was afraid to go out at night!

She said, "I got there at about 3 o'clock in the morning. I put the key in the latch, but I felt so good that I took it back out and walked the streets all night long saying, 'Devil, you're a liar. I'm not afraid of you anymore!'"

God delivered her from fear! If you are bound with a spirit of fear, He wants to do the same thing for you. You don't have to be afraid anymore. You can turn around and face the enemy with confidence because God is on your side!

Let me pray for you:

Father, in Jesus' name, I come to You on behalf of this one that's bound by fear. Thank You for the authority You've given me over devils. Fear, you foul tormenting

spirit, I adjure you by Jesus — Loose your hold on this person's life. I command it in the name of Jesus. Lord, give them a miracle of deliverance, and give them the strength to stand up against the enemy. In Jesus' name, I call it done. Amen and amen.

11
SINGER GETS HIS BIG BREAK

Glenn grew up in the inner-city neighborhood of Washington, D.C. As soon as he discovered his natural gift for singing, he saw it as his ticket out of the ghetto. He believed his musical career was the answer for him.

At age 13, he began singing for local events. A little recognition eventually led to area, statewide, and national performances. One night, he saw five men singing on the Ed Sullivan Show. This group, The Temptations, made a big impression on him. He began to study them, dress like them, and sing like them.

By the time he was working with his third musical group, The Temptations had heard about Glenn and offered him a spot. He had finally made it.

It wasn't long before Glenn Leonard was singing lead. Yet, this man noticed a void in the core of his being. He was always seeking the adrenaline rush, but it would soon fade when the concert or recording session was over. The entertainer began looking for his next thrills in drugs, alcohol and women.

One day, Glenn quit the group he had idolized for so long and began a solo career. He threw a three-day bash of drugs and alcohol to celebrate his brand new solo release. On the last night of his binge, the oppression of his emptiness reached an all-time low. He kicked all his party friends out of his hotel room and in his despair turned on the television to drown out the tormenting thoughts in his mind. He had no more alternatives, no more answers. Little did he know, he was at a turning point in his life.

"At the end of three days," Glenn remembers, "I was alone in a hotel room. A thought came to mind, 'What's gonna make this time different?' Fear came over me and I turned on the TV. It was in the wee hours of the morning. As I flipped through the channels, I heard a man's voice. The man shouted at me from across the television."

As you might have guessed, that man was this same Holy Ghost preacher that Pastor Paul had heard on those records — Schambach! During that sermon, the Lord moved on my heart and I said, "You, sitting in that hotel room. God has his hand on your life, son! Jesus is the One you are looking for!"

Then Glenn Leonard's miracle took place. It felt like somebody else was in that hotel room with him. It was the Holy Ghost! He had a supernatural encounter - the presence of Almighty God filled his room. Then, suddenly, after three days and nights of cocaine, marijuana, and champagne, he was finally sober.

Exhilarated by this unexplainable supernatural experience, Glenn drove home to his wife and children. Immediately, he sought out a friend who had become a Christian. That friend led him to Jesus Christ and within 15 minutes, Glenn was filled with the Holy Ghost. This happened on March 8, 1984.

His wife had been on the verge of leaving him. His new start not only set him free from despair, but God put His family back together, too.

The last time Glenn Leonard testified in one of my meetings, he and his wife and family were ministers of the Gospel. Instead of singing for The Temptations or for the devil, Brother Leonard is leading people to their new lives in Jesus Christ!

CONCLUSION
"HE'LL DO IT FOR YOU"

Do you need a miracle of deliverance today? I know God will do it for you if you'll let Him. I don't care what your situation is. I don't care how many times you've tried and blown it.

There are no "lost causes" in God's eyes; there are no irreversible situations. There is hope for every alcoholic, drug addict, liar, cheater, adulterer, murderer or prostitute. It does not matter what the crime is. When a man or woman repents, a change takes place. That old hardened criminal may deserve eternity in hell, but when he receives Jesus as Lord and Savior of his life, he becomes a child of God who will live in Heaven forever with Him. Hallelujah! What a miracle!

My miracle came on a street corner in Harrisburg, Pennsylvania. As I rushed by on the way from work, I heard the voice of a street-corner preacher.

"Hey, sinner!"

I stopped dead in my tracks. "Who knows me around here," I thought. You see, I knew I was a sinner.

So I leaned against a light pole and heard the preacher tell of Christ's love for me. He explained the plan of salvation for about 15 minutes. I learned that Jesus would forgive my past life of sin, and give me complete cleansing in exchange. The Holy Spirit let me know, I had no other way of being free from my sin.

There on that street corner, I fell to my knees, made an altar out of a curb and surrendered my heart to Jesus Christ. People walking by laughed at me, but I didn't care.

Now, I didn't know the theological term for what happened to me; it just felt like I had taken a shower on the inside.

God wants to do the same thing for you.

Jesus said, *"Unless one is born again, he cannot see the kingdom of God." (John 3:3)* You must be born again!

I'm not talking about shaking a preacher's hand or putting your name on some church book. You might as well shake a donkey's tail and put your name on a barn door!

The only way to be saved is through Jesus Christ. Buddha is not the way. Mohammed is not the way. Hari Krishna is not the way. I'll take it one step further. The Virgin Mary is not the way! Jesus is the Only Way. He is The Way, The Truth and The Life.

There is no purgatory. You're either saved or you're lost. You're either going to make heaven your home or you'll split Hell wide open. I know folks don't want to hear this kind of preaching. The church has changed its message. 'Do the best you can. It'll all come out in the wash.' You lying devil! It's not coming out in any wash. There's only one thing that can wash your sins away, and that is the blood of Jesus Christ!

This is the miracle of salvation. The blood of Jesus can wash away every sin! Romans 10:9 says, *"That if you confess with your mouth the Lord Jesus and believe in your heart that God has raised Him from the dead, you will be saved."*

If you want this miracle of salvation to take place in your life, then repeat this prayer after me:

Father, in Jesus' name, I come to you as a sinner. I confess my sin. I repent of my sin. I turn my back on sin. I've made up my mind that I'm going to serve the Lord and make heaven my home. Lord, I'm weak. I confess that to You. Make an entrance into my life by Your Spirit. Walk in me. Talk in me. Be my God, and let me be Your child. I believe in my heart, and I confess with my mouth that You raised Jesus from the dead. Lord, You said if I believe that and confess it, I'm saved. Thank you, Lord, for saving me. Amen and amen.

Now, if you prayed that prayer, then I believe you are a child of God. I want you to write to me and let me know, because I have a booklet I want to send you absolutely free. It's called *You're One in a Million.* Request it when you write. It will tell you about the commitment you just made to God, and it will help you in your daily Christian walk with Him.

Glory to God! I hope these testimonies of deliverance have blessed your heart. But we're not done yet. Oh, no. We're just getting started!

MIRACLES
OF HEALING

INTRODUCTION
"THE LESSER IS INCLUDED IN THE GREATER"

As we have seen, the greatest miracle that can take place in an individual's life is when God reaches down His strong arm into the pit of sin, picks up a sinner and washes him in the blood of Jesus Christ.

Now, I have learned in the science of logic that the lesser is included in the greater. That means if the greatest miracle is the salvation of the soul, then all the other lesser miracles are included! If you can have faith for salvation, you can have faith for anything else that you may need. I believe this with all my heart.

Jesus Christ not only died on the cross to take away our sins, but He also took stripes on His back for our physical healing. Salvation and healing go hand in hand. You can't preach one without the other. If you preach salvation, you've got to preach divine healing.

In John 5:1-9, we read a great story of Jesus working a miracle of healing. Read it with me.

"After this there was a feast of the Jews, and Jesus went up to Jerusalem. Now there is in Jerusalem by the Sheep Gate a pool, which is called in Hebrew, Bethesda, having five porches. In these lay a great multitude of sick people, blind, lame, paralyzed, waiting for the moving of the water. For an angel went down at a certain time into the pool and stirred up the water; then whoever stepped in first, after the stirring of the water, was made well of whatever disease he had. Now a certain man was there who had an infirmity thirty-eight years. When Jesus saw him lying there, and knew that he already had been in that condition a long

time, He said to him, 'Do you want to be made well?' The sick man answered Him, 'Sir, I have no man to put me into the pool when the water is stirred up; but while I am coming, another steps down before me.' Jesus said to him, 'Rise, take up your bed and walk.' And immediately the man was made well, took up his bed, and walked."

This is the story of a man who was sick and diseased for thirty-eight long years, waiting for the troubling of the waters at the pool of Bethesda. In the Hebrew, Bethesda means "the house of mercy."

People brought the sick, the diseased, the blind, the maimed and the dumb to this special place for just one purpose...for the troubling of the waters. When the angel stirred the water, the race was on! The person who moved fastest and reached the water the quickest would be made whole. And this poor man...

"I have no one to help me," he told Jesus. "There is always somebody pushing right by me to get into the water first!"

The heart of Jesus went out to this man. So Jesus commanded the man to "rise, take up your bed and walk." Immediately (I love that word "immediately"!), the man was made whole and walked. Even though he had been bound with this infirmity for thirty-eight years, he was made whole instantly when Jesus spoke to him.

Jesus is a compassionate Savior. If the doctors have given up hope, and we cannot find one person to agree with us in prayer — Jesus is available. He gives hope to the hopeless. I have been an eyewitness to so many great miracles of healing throughout my ministry. A lot of folks may say He does not do it anymore. Let them talk all they want. I know He is still doing it because I have seen it with my own eyes.

Maybe you need a healing touch from God right now. I believe that as you read these next few stories, God is going to trouble the waters. The Holy Ghost is going to stir faith in your heart. Let that faith come alive inside of you, and get ready to receive your own miracle from God.

I'm so thankful that we serve a God who heals! He is Jehovah Rapha! He is our healer!

12
I DIED ON AN OPERATING TABLE

I believe that God has a miracle for everyone who is sick. A lot of folks don't like this idea. They say, "Well, God put it on you to make you humble."

God doesn't put sickness on anybody! It's the devil that puts it on you. But God is going to take it off of you.

Still, there are skeptics. They might say, "Preacher, it's easy for you to *tell* people that God's going to heal them. But do you really know what they're going through?"

Well I've got a story for the skeptics. I myself am a living testimony of the saving, healing, miracle-working power of God!

In 1987, my health was in serious jeopardy. I was facing quintuple bypass surgery for my heart. The doctor's told me I wouldn't be able to preach anymore, and if I did I'd have to preach sitting down.

They shook their heads when they examined my X-rays; the blockage was extensive - 87% blockage in one artery, 98% in another, 99% in yet another. My young doctor couldn't believe I was able to walk across the room, much less preach the way I do.

As someone who had preached faith and never taken aspirin, facing such a surgery was a frightening experience. I remember calling in my wife and grown children on the eve of the surgery. I couldn't predict the outcome, but we prayed and placed my health in the hands of the One who had been my Great Physician throughout my life.

Much later on, after the surgery, I found out that God had placed His ministering angels throughout the hospital. Spirit-filled nurses and attendants were stationed in the prep room, in surgery, in intensive care and in recovery. When they saw I was in their unit, they prayed and interceded for me. All through that time of great testing, God was in control.

During surgery, I died on that operating table! It took the doctors almost five minutes to get my heart functioning again. My doctor, Dr. Cherry, didn't tell me this initially because he thought it might impede my recovery.

But when I later learned these things, I realized that God wasn't finished with me yet. He still had plans for me.

During my six-month recovery process, I had to learn new rest patterns and eating habits, and began exercising regularly. These are other ways in which I can treat the Lord's "temple" with respect. Even though I didn't drink alcohol or smoke, I had harmed my body through overeating, eating the wrong kinds of foods and neglecting regular exercise.

Formerly, I thought all I had to do was pray over my food and keep on working for the Lord. Thank God for the new lessons I learned; and I also thank Him for His grace.

You see, after I started feeling better, I became a little careless. I started to let go of the rest patterns; I just worked harder. I didn't exercise as often - I let my flesh get the best of me. We must be faithful to care for the gift of life we've been given. God will do what we can't do.

About seven years after open-heart surgery, another illness hit - congestive heart failure. When Dr. Cherry called me into his office and I sat across from him, he was so pale he looked like he needed a doctor. He said, "Brother Schambach, you are going to have to stop preaching for a while. We need a miracle if you will ever preach again." He said I had lost a significant amount of my heart's functioning capacity and my body had filled up with fluid.

I don't mind telling you, that news hit me hard. The devil brought all kinds of thoughts to mind. He kept poking his ugly finger at me with thoughts of failure and death.

So, I would just talk back to the devil. "You've been a liar from the beginning, devil. I'm not finished yet. I'm just getting started! I'm in this for the long haul."

You see, if I really thought I wasn't going to preach anymore, I'd ask God to take me on home. This is what I was born for - to preach the gospel. But I knew that God was not done with me yet. I knew he still had plans for my ministry.

So even though Dr. Cherry pulled me off the road for three months, I got busy at home. I sent a letter to everyone I knew asking for prayer. Some preachers try to hide what they go through. But I hurt. I bleed. And I needed help. I wrote to my mailing list and said, "I've been praying for you for 40 years. Now I want some of it back. Pray for me." And they started praying.

I called every prayer line I could find. I wanted every bit of prayer I could muster up. Corporate prayer is a powerful tool against the devil. God cannot ignore the prayers of His people. As a result of the petitions to the Almighty, something supernatural happened.

I was scheduled for a visit to the doctor after three months of rest. I went back to Dr. Cherry and sat across from him. He looked a different color this time! He explained that with congestive heart failure, the best doctors can hope for is to maintain the level of failure without the heart losing any more of its functioning. Never with congestive heart failure do doctors see an increase in functioning.

Well, I've always served a God of the miraculous. Not only had my heart merely increased in functioning, it had increased 65%! Dr. Cherry told my board members that he had seen many miracles, but mine was the greatest miracle he had ever seen.

He released me to go anywhere in the world! Anywhere! I don't have to slow down my pace. In fact, it's the younger people who work with me who have a hard time keeping up with my pace!

Praise God! The effectual, fervent prayers of God's people make a difference.

13
BOY BORN BLIND HEALED THROUGH RADIO

A number of years ago, we were considering taking the "Voice of Power" off of the air in Chicago. I had a memo on my desk about it. All I had to do was sign the paper and it would be done. But something kept me from doing this. God said, "Not now."

Well, I decided I was not going to argue with the voice of God. Am I ever glad!

Around that time, there was a young Jewish boy in Chicago who had been blind from birth. He often sat at home and listened to Rock 'n Roll music on the radio. But one day as he twisted the radio dial, a different kind of message came on, and it caught his attention.

The man on the radio was talking about Jesus, and how he had restored sight to a blind man. The man then proceeded to pray for everyone listening who was blind. "I'm praying that your blind eyes will be opened right now by the power of God!"

Suddenly, the boy's eyes cleared up!

He dashed into the hallway of his home, shouting, "Mama! Mama! I can see!"

His mother stared in amazement. She wondered how this could have happened. The little boy tried to explain to her what had happened, and went to show her the radio preacher, but the program was over by then

So the next morning at the same time, they both sat down together by the radio, spinning through the channels until the little boy heard the voice of the same man who had prayed for him the day before.

"That's the one! That's the man!"

That program was my "Voice of Power" broadcast that I had almost taken off the air!

The boy's mother wrote me a letter and told me the whole story. I thought about the memo on my desk. Needless to say, I decided to continue airing the Voice of Power in the Chicago area.

14
THE LIVING ROOM MIRACLE

My ministry is not only broadcast on radio, but is also extended to television. In fact, the "Power Today" telecast can be seen in every nation of the world. Think of this. Every nation of the world!

That gets me excited, because the Bible says that this gospel will be preached in all of the world as a witness, and then the end shall come. So to think that we're getting the gospel out into every part of the earth just blesses me. I know that Jesus is coming back soon!

A lot of folks can't make it to my meetings, so we bring the meetings right into their living rooms. Many are saved, healed, delivered and set free because of the message they hear and see on their television. I'll share one such story with you.

Karol was a woman in despair. She had found out from the doctors that she had 3 tumors in her left breast.

I tell you, folks, I know what it's like to get a bad report from the doctor. When that happens, it's all you can think about. The devil comes on the scene and puts all kinds of thoughts in your head like, "You're going to die!" or "God will never heal you!"

But God had a miracle in store for Karol.

One night, she was sitting in her living room, watching my television program. As she listened to the message, faith started rising up inside her.

At the end of my programs, I always pray the prayer of faith. The Bible says, "The prayer of faith shall save the sick." I believe this, so I never miss an opportunity to pray for people, that the Lord will heal them and set them free.

At the time, the Lord moved on my heart to do something as I prayed.

"If no one is there to lay hands on you," I told my audience, "put your hand on your body where you need a healing."

Then I prayed.

In obedience to the man of God, Karol put her hand on her body during the prayer. She felt the presence of Almighty God in that living room. Immediately, she knew she was healed.

She went back to the doctor and told him she was healed.

"I want another X-ray," she said.

Now, you know how some doctors are. They think they are the only ones that do the healing. But I don't care what they say. My God is the Great Physician! He can do anything!

When Karol told the doctor this, he said, "You're crazy for believing you are healed!"

But she didn't let that deter her faith. She knew she was healed!

So the doctor reluctantly did the tests. To his amazement, when the results came back, there were no tumors. It was confirmed. The tumors were totally gone!

When I had my tent up in Phoenix, this dear sister came up to the platform and testified about how the Lord had healed her.

Praise God! That's why I love bringing the Word of God to people through television. They can't come up and walk through a prayer line, but they can put their faith to work when they hear the Word preached in their home, and God can perform a miracle.

15
DOUBLY GOOD

I love it when a doctor examines somebody that he said had cancer, and after prayer they can't find it. I love to see the doctor scratching his head when the power of God throws a wrench in all his medical knowledge.

"And my speech and my preaching were not with persuasive words of human wisdom, but in demonstration of the Spirit and of power, that your faith should not be in the wisdom of men but in the power of God." *(1 Corinthians 2:4-5)*

This is what I preach. I don't fill people's heads with elegant words. Too many preachers spend all their time telling God's people about things. I like to SHOW them. I like to demonstrate the gospel of power. I love to see those doctors scratching their heads.

Now, there are many doctors who are men of faith. God uses them in their field, I know. But I believe God likes to amaze even the doctors. He likes to let them know that He's still God — that He's the Great Physician.

In Hobbema, Alberta, Canada, I preached the Word of God on an Indian Reservation. I was encouraging the people to give to God.

I'll never forget this one Indian brother who was there. He had his daughter with him, who was diagnosed with cancer of the cervix. That night he gave to God. He made a faith promise, believing that God would meet his financial need and heal his daughter.

The next day, he called me at the motel I was staying in. It was the only one in town.

He said, "Brother Schambach."

I said, "Who is this?"

"I was in your service yesterday," he replied. "I just had to call you."

I wondered how he knew where I was. I asked him, "How did you find me?"

He said, "There's only one motel in this town. I knew you had to be here since you're not at the tent. They put me through to you. I just had to tell you something. I made that faith promise and gave to God. I was obedient to what you said. Well, I went to work this morning and my employer put a $20,000 check in my hand!"

He woke me up! I said, "Hold the phone while I shout with you a little bit!"

While I was shouting he said, "Now, don't get too carried away. I'm not done yet. My daughter, who had cancer of the cervix, went back to the doctor. And he's scratching his head. He said, 'I don't know where the cancer's gone, but the cancer has disintegrated in a matter of 24 hours.'"

That's greater than $20,000. That's greater than all the money in the world!

These are the kinds of miracles that God is doing. It's the manifestation of His Spirit in this Last Day. I call it 'exhibition.' I like that word. Preachers of the Gospel must place the power of the Living God on exhibition. It's time we exercise our faith and demonstrate this power that we have been given!

16
CHAIN REACTION

I have a dear friend, Brother Alvaro Fernandez, a Latin-American brother who lives in Norway. He and his wife have been such a blessing to my ministry. When we held revival meetings in Russia, it was Brother Fernandez that coordinated the whole thing.

It blesses me to see young ministers like him walking in faith and doing the works of Christ across the globe. But that faith of his was put to the test a number of years ago. The devil wanted to rob him, but God performed a miracle.

Eight months after he and his wife, Elizabeth, were married, the doctors discovered that she had a tumor on her lungs. She went into extensive chemotherapy to treat the cancer. The doctors didn't give her much hope. This was a very difficult time for both of them.

It was during this time that I asked Brother Fernandez to help me with my Russian Crusade. He agreed, and began the work. His wife, although very sick, didn't stay in bed. She went with him. She had to wear a turban on her head because of the chemotherapy.

In May of that year, I met them in Russia. I prayed for that dear woman, and you know what? God healed her! Three months later, the doctors took another test. The tumor was totally gone, and all that remained was a mark inside where it had been. The doctors said it was as if someone had removed the cancer from her body. Hallelujah! I know who that 'Someone' was. It was Jesus Christ!

But that wasn't all God had in store.

The chemotherapy had damaged Elizabeth's womb so badly that she could not have any children. The doctors said it would be impossible. Well, they were wrong.

One year later, Brother and Sister Fernandez visited the U.S. When I saw them, I laid hands on her again. "I bless the fruit of this womb."

Now, they were perplexed by this, since the doctors had told her she could not have any children. But I serve a God that likes to confound the doctors!

When they went back to Norway, Elizabeth was feeling a little strange. So the doctors took a picture of her womb. To their amazement, something was there!

They couldn't believe this, so they started checking her for cancer again. But, glory to God, it wasn't cancer! It was a baby!

Now they have two precious children, Samuel and Victoria Joy. God has blessed that family for their faithfulness to Him.

But the story is not over yet!

Some time later, it was discovered that Elizabeth had a form of heart disease. You know, that devil just can't take a hint! You think he'd learn by now that he can't put his filthy hands on God's people and get away with it. God had another miracle waiting in the wings.

When they discovered that she had heart disease, they sent notice to me. I was conducting meetings in Long Island at the time. So I sent a prayer cloth to them (see Acts 19:11-12). Now, I'll talk about prayer cloths more a little later.

When the prayer cloth touched her, she was totally healed and restored. And God did more than just that! While she was in the hospital, she was reading my first *Miracles* book. She gave it to the lady in the bed beside her to read. When that lady read those stories of God's miracle-working power, she got saved and was healed of her infirmity!

See, the devil doesn't have any sense. What he intended for evil, God worked out for good. God set off a chain reaction for Brother and Sister Fernandez. He just kept on working miracles! You see, it doesn't matter what the report of the doctors is. What matters is the report of the Lord. If He says you are healed, then you *ARE* healed!

17
WHAT THE BEST DOCTORS COULDN'T DO

If the devil can't get to you, sometimes he goes after your family. A family emergency can knock the wind out of even the greatest man of faith, and the devil knows that. He doesn't care how he gets you. He'll just try to pull you down whatever way he can.

In 1993, the devil went after the family of a dear brother, Reverend Joe Martin, who pastored a church in Virginia Beach, Virginia, where I was conducting a ten-day tent crusade.

Brother Martin sponsored these meetings. He had been preparing for four hectic weeks. So by the time the crusade rolled around, he and his wife, Kathy, and their eight children were exhausted (his wife was pregnant with their ninth child also).

On October 7, the night before the crusade began, their eighteen-month-old daughter, Elisha Ann, started having difficulty breathing. She started coughing with something like a whooping cough. Her parents thought it was just a bad cold, so they passed it off for a while.

By Sunday night, the problem had grown more severe, and they noticed a rattle in her lungs. She could hardly breathe, and couldn't drink milk. So they took her to the doctor the next morning.

There were four specialists at the hospital at the time. They listened to her lungs and looked at her heart on a special heart sonogram. The doctors just looked at each other in silence, and then told the father how serious it was.

"This is not bronchitis. This is not a whooping cough. Your daughter has a congenital heart defect, a cardiac myopathy, and all four chambers of the heart have failed. This is blood in her lungs. One third of the patients with such a heart defect have heart transplants or die, one third stay the same with medicine and one third get better."

They told him that his daughter would live on increasing doses of medicine until she died unless she had a heart transplant.

"You're wrong," Brother Martin told them.

Then all four specialists looked him in the eye. "I wish we could say we're wrong, but we all agree."

So they took their little daughter back to the tent just before the service started. I was in my trailer. Brother Martin walked in crying and told me about it. "Brother Schambach, she's going to be the first one over the ramp. You're going to lay hands on her on this children's blessing night, and she'll be the first one healed."

"That's exactly right," I said.

You know, I think that little Elisha is the reason that I was sent to that town in the first place. The second I laid hands on her that night, she began to recover. Praise God! As they were driving home that night, Elisha drank a whole bottle in three minutes, which she hadn't done in four whole days. The rattle in her breathing was gone as well.

The next morning they went back to the same doctors. Within a short period of time, they all agreed that her heart was normal. There was no leakage in any of her heart's chambers. She was totally healed! Once again, the doctors were astounded.

In the service that Wednesday night, Elisha walked across the platform smiling and waving to the people.

After four weeks they returned again to the doctor, who congratulated them and told them that she would be off all medication for the rest of her life.

Let me tell you folks, it works!

18
BLOOD TRANSFUSION FROM CALVARY

Another child I saw healed was Jonathan Gregori. But this one hit a little closer to home. Jonathan is the son of my niece, Joann. I know that many of you reading this book have loved ones that need a healing touch from God. Well, we preachers are no different. Sometimes we have great needs within our own families.

At age three, Jonathan came down with a blood disease - I.T.P. The platelets in his blood were being destroyed, and within a twenty-four hour period, there were black and blue bruises all over his body.

His parents didn't know what was happening to him, so they took him to the doctor. This particular doctor, when he examined Jonathan, just blurted out, "Oh, your son has leukemia." (The disease he had was very similar to leukemia.) This devastated Jonathan's parents.

It wasn't long before the boy was in the hospital and was put on heavy medication. They had to pad his crib because the disease caused him to bruise very easily.

It was during that time that I brought the big gospel tent into that area of the Bronx, New York. One night we had a children's blessing service. My main emphasis that night was healing. And I'll never forget Jonathan's father, Pastor Mark Gregori, bringing him up to the front to be prayed for.

I took the boy from his father's arms and held him. Then I prayed over him, "Give him a blood transfusion from Calvary! In Jesus' name."

Within that same week, Jonathan's platelets came to the right level. The disease was gone! There were no more bruises. He was made completely whole!

Jonathan is a grown man now, and God's using him in His service. He has traveled to several other countries as a missionary. He is a marvelous example of God's healing power that is still at work today.

19
GINGER STANDS PROXY

In an earlier chapter I talked about 'proxy' - standing in the place of someone else and agreeing for God to touch them. That can be for a loved one to get saved, like in the "Broken Needles" story. But it can also be for a loved one's healing. You can read such a story in John's gospel, when Jesus healed the nobleman's son.

'So Jesus came again to Cana of Galilee where He had made the water wine. And there was a certain nobleman whose son was sick at Capernaum. When he heard that Jesus had come out of Judea into Galilee, he went to Him and implored Him to come down and heal his son, for he was at the point of death. Then Jesus said to him, 'Unless you people see signs and wonders, you will by no means believe.' The nobleman said to Him, 'Sir, come down before my child dies!' Jesus said to him, 'Go your way; your son lives.' So the man believed the word that Jesus spoke to him, and he went his way. And as he was now going down, his servants met him and told him, saying, 'Your son lives!' Then he inquired of them the hour when he got better. And they said to him, 'Yesterday at the seventh hour the fever left him.' So the father knew that it was at the same hour in which Jesus said to him, 'Your son lives.' And he himself believed, and his whole household." **(John 4:46-53)**

What an unusual story! Jesus came back to the very area where he turned the water into wine, and a certain man came to Him. This is proxy. He came to stand proxy for his son, who was home, six to nine hours away.

He came to Jesus saying, "Sir, my boy's at the point of death. Come along home with me and heal him."

(Ah, everybody would like to take Him home with them.)

Jesus gave him a gentle rebuke and said, "Unless you see signs and wonders, you will not believe." At another time Jesus said, *"Blessed are those that have not seen, and yet have believed." (John 20:29)*

Jesus says the same to you and me today! We don't have to see it to believe it. All we've got to do is hear what the Word of God has to say about it and stand on that Word, and God will bring it to pass. Hallelujah!

After Jesus gave his rebuke, he said to the man, "Your son lives." He didn't go home with him. All he did was speak the word, and the man believed what Jesus spoke to him. So he went his way.

Now here is where the devil likes to gain advantage. When you leave the presence of God and you go home to a boy that's dying, all kinds of thoughts go through your mind. "You're too late! Your boy is gonna die!" You lying devil! I believe what Jesus said. I believe that my son lives!

When that man got home, he found his little boy totally healed. This is a great example of standing proxy for someone else. I've seen God do many outstanding miracles by proxy.

A woman named Ginger put this thing to work.

In 1998, I held a crusade in Newark, New Jersey. I announced to the people that I was going to have 'proxy night.'

I said, "If you have a loved one in a hospital, you come on proxy night and pray for them, and they're going to be healed."

Ginger heard the word that I spoke. Her sister Kathy had been critically injured in a motorcycle accident. She was in a semi-comatose state known as post-traumatic amnesia, and wasn't expected to live. She had terrible brain damage. The look of death was all over her.

The doctors told Ginger that if her sister ever woke up from the coma, that she would be incapacitated. They said she'd never walk, talk, read or write again. They said she would not remember who anyone was.

But thank God, Ginger did not believe the report of the doctors. She believed the report of the Lord. She took me up on my challenge. When proxy night came, she came ready to agree for her sister.

As I preached that night, the anointing of God was all over the tent. Jesus showed up! Hallelujah! And I told the people, "You've got to tell the Lord what you want!"

You see, I believe that when we pray, we should tell the Lord exactly what we want. We can't just sit back and say, "Well, I'll take whatever the Lord wants to give me." We've got to tell God exactly what we want.

When I said this, Ginger thought about Kathy.

"I want my sister back!" she thought.

I called people up to walk across the ramp for prayer. Before we even got a chance to lay hands on her, she fell out under the power of God.

Her faith was strong. She believed the report of the Lord, and was convinced that her sister was healed. Now, this miracle didn't take place at that exact moment, like when Jesus prayed for the nobleman's son. He had something else in mind that would absolutely blow the mind of the doctor.

Ginger went back to this doctor, whose name was Eileen.

"Look, Ginger, I'd love to tell you that they just snap out of it. I'd love to tell you they just get better - like I'll walk down the hall and she'll just be sitting there saying, 'Hey, Eileen. How are you doing?' It just doesn't happen."

But all the time, Ginger was sitting there thinking, "Oh, yes it does. Yes it does."

So the next day, this doctor was walking down the halls of the ward. As she walked past Kathy's room, she heard a voice.

"Hey, Eileen. How are you doing?" she said. That girl was out of a coma, totally healed and restored by the power of God. I don't know what that Dr. Eileen did after that, but I know that she couldn't deny the power of God.

That's what proxy is all about. We can be in perfect agreement regarding the promises of God, exercise our faith and watch God work!

20
THERE'S NO FAITH LIKE A MAMA'S FAITH

Mama, don't ever give up praying. You might feel like God isn't hearing your prayer. The devil might tell you that your baby's never going to get saved or healed. But the devil is a liar! When he tells you that, start shouting. God is going to perform a miracle for your child.

There truly is no faith like a mama's faith.

I told you earlier about a mother who prayed for her son's salvation. Now here are a couple of stories about mothers who brought their children to my meetings, in full assurance that God was going to heal them.

A brother named Fiifi was born with a skin condition. He had eczema all over his body, especially on his face and hands. These areas broke out like rashes. Sometimes they were so bad that his eyelashes and eyebrows fell out.

When the boy was five years old, his mother Elizabeth brought him to one of my meetings. She believed that the Lord would totally heal him of this skin condition.

As I preached, faith began to stir in Fiifi's heart.

You know, Jesus said in Matthew 18 that unless you *"become as little children, you shall not enter into the kingdom of heaven."* There's just something about a child that knows how to believe God.

When I called for the offering, the little boy walked up to the front with a dollar bill. His mother walked alongside him. She prayed silently, "Lord, I wish Brother Schambach would touch him." But she didn't say anything.

Fiifi brought his offering up, and when I saw him, I reached out and touched that awful rash on his face.

Of course, his mother was overjoyed. "Thank you, Lord," she whispered.

The miracle had already begun. Within a few days, the rashes all over Fiifi's body had completely disappeared. They have never returned!

Crystal was another mother who believed God for her son's healing.

When her son was three years of age, he lost use of his arm. At first they thought it was arthritis. But one day, as he was walking his legs gave out also.

They brought him to the hospital. After running some tests, the doctors said he had a tumor along his spinal cord.

So they started radiation therapy. Every day for three months, that little boy had to go through extensive treatment. He had two surgeries in the process. In one of them, they actually lost him for a while.

Things looked very bleak. The doctors only gave him a year to live.

But Crystal didn't lose her faith. She cried out to God for her son, and prayed that he would send someone of faith to pray for the boy.

Now, she had followed my ministry for about 16 years, so when she heard that I was coming to that area, her faith started to soar. God had answered her prayer. She thought, "If I could just get him to the man of God, he will be healed."

The night she brought him, the Lord directed me to call specifically all those who were terminally ill with cancer. Crystal wheeled her son up to the front for prayer.

Soon, he began to recover. The doctors had given him one year to live. Well, he is still going strong! He's a healthy boy now and says he's going to preach when he grows up. I like that! And it all started with the faith of that mother who wouldn't let the devil steal her child.

21
FORTY TUMORS AND A HANDKERCHIEF

Sometimes we must exercise our faith for "special miracles."

As mentioned in *Acts 19:11-12:*

"And God wrought special miracles by the hands of Paul: So that from his body were brought unto the sick handkerchiefs or aprons, and the diseases departed from them, and the evil spirits went out of them." (KJV)

Paul traveled continually from place to place as he ministered. People were healed and delivered from the power of evil spirits. As a result, news of this power spread all over the country.

There were multitudes of people who needed healing and deliverance who couldn't get to him so the Spirit of the Lord instructed him to take cloths from his body and send them to those in need.

The anointing of God's power on those cloths was so strong that the people who received them were healed and delivered. The cloth became a faith trigger, a power release for special miracles.

Like Paul, I wear cloths on my body. God promised me that as I wore these pieces of cloth on my body, the same anointing that was on me as I ministered would penetrate these cloths, and they would become anointed cloths.

There is no magic in the cloth. We all wear cloth, so if there was magic in it, we'd all be healed already. That prayer cloth serves as a point of contact, allowing me to unite my faith with those who are in need.

I know some of you think prayer cloths are a bit strange. But God's Word specifically ordains their use. And that's good enough for me. If the Bible told me to stand on my head to receive my miracle, I'd do it!

I was preaching in Philadelphia one year. After the service, a woman named Arlene came to me with a strange question. She asked me if she could have my handkerchief. So I gave it to her.

What I didn't know was that Arlene had learned from the doctors that she had forty cancerous tumors in her breast.

But her faith in God was strong. When she was watching me preach, she saw me take my handkerchief out and wipe the sweat from my brow. That made her think of the scripture in Acts that we just read. She asked me for my handkerchief and I gave it to her.

One year later I was holding a tent crusade in Philadelphia. Wouldn't you know, this same woman came to the platform with a testimony. She told the people about the special miracle that God performed.

"With over forty cancerous tumors in my breast, I was facing either radiation treatments or a total mastectomy. Then, Brother Schambach came to town and I went to his meeting. As he preached, I watched him take his handkerchief out and wipe his brow, and I thought of the scripture about Paul's handkerchiefs being laid on the sick and they recovered.

"After the meeting, I asked Brother Schambach if I could have his handkerchief. The moment he handed it to me, I felt God's anointing go all through my body...and I was healed! That happened last year, and since then I have had several body scans, with no trace of cancer."

Arlene still carries that handkerchief with her everywhere she goes, and just keeps on praising the Lord for what He did for her.

22
OTHER SPECIAL MIRACLES

I actually send out prayer cloths through the mail. I send out hundreds of them every month — absolutely free. People who need a special miracle from God write or call, requesting a cloth as a point of contact for their faith.

I want to tell you about two women in particular who asked me for prayer cloths and received their miracles through faith in the living Christ.

Pauline was very sick. She had a seven-inch split inside her stomach wall, and the leakage of fluids caused third degree burns on several of her other organs. Her condition became so bad that she went into a coma.

The doctors told her sister, Wanda, to bring the family in the next day for a final visit. They thought that Pauline was going to die.

But Wanda was not going to accept it.

Now, I was in Brooklyn at the time. Wanda contacted an associate of mine who was with me, asking for a handkerchief for her sister. She wanted something that I had worn on my body while I preached. So we sent one to her right away.

God honored her faith. Within hours of receiving the cloth, Pauline began responding. She came out of that coma, healed by the power of God.

Both Pauline and Wanda came up to the platform during one of my meetings to testify about what the Lord had done. Doctors had told her she wouldn't live, but there she was in front of me giving God praise.

Another great prayer cloth story was told to me by Chris Holland, a woman from Georgia.

Her father was diagnosed with melanoma, stage four. He had cancer all over his body. His condition was so severe, that the doctors would not even operate on him. He was told he had 6 months to live.

But this man believed in the healing power of Christ. He respectfully told the doctor, "I appreciate everything you've done for me. But now I'm going to take it to the Great Physician."

When Chris found out about her father's infirmity, she got on the phone and called every ministry she knew, including mine. When we received her call, we sent her a prayer cloth, which she immediately mailed to her dad. When he got it, he taped it to his stomach, believing that God would heal him. After he wore it like that for several days, he put it in his wallet.

Both Chris and her father were people of faith, so they stood on God's Word, believing that the healing would come. And sure enough, God came through. The man's cancer began to disappear.

He had a huge tumor on his arm. It was purple. But that tumor began to shrink. They watched it get smaller and smaller. The purple color went away. He was healed before their very eyes. The miracle was visible, so nobody could deny the power of God, and nobody could doubt it. Hallelujah! They put faith to work.

Remember, this is not magic. Our faith is not in the cloth. Our faith is in God. When you and I agree in prayer, the cloth becomes the point of contact for our faith.

Maybe you are in need of a special miracle from God. I would love to send you a prayer cloth absolutely free. My address is at the back of this book. You can contact my ministry, and I will send you a prayer cloth right away for your need.

23
A MIRACLE IN PROGRESS

Not every miracle happens instantaneously. Some miracles are progressive. They don't happen all at once.

I saw this first-hand in Canada, when I put my tent up on the Indian reservation in Hobbema, Alberta.

There was a 17-year old girl in the audience named Billie Dee. The doctors had told her she had all kinds of sicknesses. She could barely move, and didn't go to school for three months. God delivered her from these infirmities there at the tent service.

But there was one thing left that God had not healed, and she came back to the tent the next night ready to receive this final miracle.

When I had my testimony time before the message, she and her mother came across the platform and told the people how God had healed her. I was thrilled to hear the testimony.

But before they left the platform, they had another request from God.

She had lost a lot of her vision because of the sickness. She was going blind. When she was healed, part of it had been restored. But she was believing God for all of it to be restored. They told me this right there on the platform. That's faith!

So I looked at them and said, "You don't have to wait for that. We can pray right now. Right here on television."

You see, I broadcast this message on television. Some preachers might be nervous about everybody watching them pray for the sick. But I love to demonstrate the power of the gospel. I like to show it, to put it on display!

I had my daughter, Donna, and another pastor join me to pray for her. We ganged up on the devil. I took her glasses off and got ready to pray. But I only got one word out!

"Father --"

Immediately I felt the power of God on that ramp. And so did she! As we had our hands on her, she just flopped like an old dish rag. It was the anointing of the Holy Ghost!

"Give her 20/20 vision! In the name of Jesus," I prayed.

I knew she wouldn't be able to talk in that state, so I had them take her off the platform.

A little later in the service, Donna came running up to me with the news that the young girl had clear vision! So we brought her back up to see what the Lord had done.

I did a little test to see how clear her vision was, and sure enough, her eyes were totally restored. She didn't need those glasses anymore.

Hallelujah! It was a progressive miracle. God worked on her a little bit at a time, but he completed His work there in that anointing-charged atmosphere, right in front of the television cameras!

24
IN THE MIDDLE OF THE NIGHT

In 1984, I spoke at a conference at Duquesne University in Pittsburgh. There was a young man in my audience that night named Michael. God performed a miracle for him that night.

But you know, not everybody who gets a miracle comes back to testify immediately. That was the case with Michael. It was 15 years before I ever heard his story. But finally, in 1999, he came back to tell what the Lord had done for him.

He had worked at a steel mill as the main operator on a particular piece of machinery. While working one day, he injured his back.

For three years, he suffered with severe back pain. The doctors finally got to the point where they considered operating on him. The only problem was, there was a 90% chance that Michael would end up in a wheelchair.

It was about this time that I came to Pittsburgh. Michael attended my meeting there on the university campus. He heard the message of faith being preached, and I prayed for him later in the service. But he wasn't healed instantly. It was later that night that his miracle came into being.

In the middle of the night, he awoke suddenly. He was scared because he thought someone else was in his home. So he just lay there, breathing quietly, when all of a sudden his back was pulled back like a rubber band.

When that happened, he heard a loud snap. He didn't believe it at first. He thought it was just a noise in the kitchen. But then he fell back asleep.

He awoke the next morning to find that the pain was gone completely, for the first time in 3 years! The doctors were amazed at what had taken place.

Now, like I said, I didn't hear about this miracle until 15 years later, when Michael came back to testify. The pain never returned. He was rejoicing and praising God for what had been done back in 1984.

25
AN UNEXPECTED TWIST

God moves in mysterious ways. Sometimes He does things that do not make sense to the natural mind. When we are being led by His Spirit, sometimes we have to step out in faith and do things that do not make sense to the natural mind.

Throughout my years of ministry, I've been led to do things that must have seemed crazy to the people around me. But if the Holy Ghost tells me to do something, I'm going to do it. I don't care what people think. That's their business. It's my job to be obedient to God and step out in faith. He'll do the rest.

I'll never forget one particular miracle God performed for a woman named Esther Bake. After many years of pain and suffering, he totally healed and restored her. But this miracle required me to do something a little unexpected.

In 1960, Esther had been involved in two automobile accidents. In the first accident, she received a fractured skull, brain damage, and a severe injury to her left leg. Not long after that, she had another accident. This time, her neck was broken in two places and her spine was chipped all the way down.

After being X-rayed seven times, she was put in traction with sand bags on either side of her head. The orthopedic specialist put her on the critical list, giving her only 72 hours to live. She did survive, but was put in a steel neck brace.

Four years after the accidents, Esther started having severe headaches and eventually went into a coma. She was admitted once again into the hospital, where the doctors found a tumor in her brain. All seemed hopeless. During one night, she felt her spirit leave her body, and was looking down at herself from above the room.

A minister came and prayed for her, though, and she did not die. That night, she came out of the coma and felt something draining down her throat. She knew she had been healed, and sure enough, when the doctors re-examined her, the tumor was gone!

But her pain remained. She took pain pills all day so she could sleep at night. Her medical bill alone was $100 a month! This was back in the 60's. That was a lot of money back then. It's a lot of money now!

On July 5, 1971, eleven years after the accidents, Esther stumbled across the Voice of Power radio broadcast. As she heard the Word of God come forth, faith came alive in her heart, and she was determined to get to one of my meetings, believing that the Lord would heal her body.

That year, the day after Thanksgiving, we put the tent up in Miami, close to where Esther lived. I'll never forget seeing her that day in that steel neck brace. She couldn't even turn her head, and had to turn her whole body to look around. But her faith was strong.

I called her down to the front.

"What did you come for?"

"I've come for a miracle," she replied.

"Then what are you doing with that steel brace on your neck? Take it off."

Now, this is back when I had a lot of guts. Under the unction of the Holy Ghost, I put my hands on her head and said, "In the name of Jesus!"

Then I twisted her head! The entire audience gasped. They must have thought this preacher had really lost it. Quite frankly, when I look back on the incident I get a little frightened. No one should ever do that unless the Holy Ghost explicitly directs that way!

To everyone's astonishment, Esther was totally healed! She started moving around more than she had in years. Glory to God!

She went back to her clinic and had the doctors X-ray her. They couldn't even find the break in her neck. Hallelujah! It was gone!

Esther came to me later with a proposition. "Brother Schambach, since God healed me, I want to give Him that $100 a month that I've been spending on medicine."

I said, "No, Esther, you don't want to do that. You've been doing without all these years. Go buy yourself a new wardrobe."

But she insisted. "I want to give it to God," she said.

"Well, okay," I said. After all, I didn't want to rob her of a blessing. "Where are you working, Esther?"

"I work for the city," she said.

"Are you the boss?"

"No, I'm just one of the girls."

"How would you like to run the place?"

Then I prayed for her. Some time after, I put my tent up in South Bay, Florida, where she came to me with another testimony.

"Brother Schambach, they elevated me! Now I am in charge of the whole office. I also got a $300 a month raise, and I can give God that $100 every month, too."

Isn't that beautiful? It was a total and complete miracle, triggered by the faith of a woman who was bold enough to trust God for the impossible.

CONCLUSION
"EVERYONE THAT ASKS"

What outstanding testimonies of God's healing power! But He's not finished yet. He is still healing the sick.

In November of 2001, we held a miracle service right on the campus of my new Global Outreach Center, my ministry headquarters. There was a woman in the crowd from Pittsburgh, Pennsylvania, who came all the way down here to get a healing touch from God.

Before I even started preaching, she was out of that wheelchair, walking and praising God. I tell you, folks, when that happened, everybody in the place started shouting. It is such a thrill to see that God is still at work.

What do you have need of? Are you oppressed by a spirit of infirmity? Do you need a healing touch from God? He's waiting to perform the miracle for you. You just have to stand on His promises and believe that He'll do it.

"For everyone who asks receives, and he who seeks finds, and to him who knocks it will be opened." (Matthew 7:8)

If God says 'everybody,' He means 'everybody!'

The devil may be attacking you with infirmity right now. Don't stand for it! You can put the devil where he belongs.

But I want you to know, everything you trust God for, you've got to fight for it. You can't sit in that upholstered pew and say, "Well, whenever the Lord gets ready He's going to drop it in my lap." He isn't going to do anything!

You're going to have to get up and stretch out on His Word and lay some footprints down. You're going to have to eyeball the devil and say, "I've had enough of this!"

Amen! You can put him where he belongs. That devil has no business on your back. He has no business in you head or in your stomach. He has no business in your feet or your legs. He has no business in your chest. There's only one place the devil has any right to be - and that's under your feet! He is a defeated foe!

I want to pray for your healing right now. I don't care what the devil has put on you, God is going to take it off of you. So let me pray for your physical condition.

Father, in Jesus' name, I come against the works of the devil. He's a thief that comes to steal, to kill and to destroy. But You said You have come that we might have life and have it more abundantly. In the name of Jesus, let resurrection power come alive. Jesus, stretch forth that nail-scarred hand and heal all manner of sickness. I curse blindness and deafness. I curse crippling spirits. I curse heart disease, cancer, back problems, and liver trouble. Satan, I adjure you by Jesus, LOOSE your hold on this individual's life. From the crown of their head to the soles of their feet to their fingertips, let that healing power come alive now. In Jesus Christ's name, and by faith I call it done. Amen and amen.

Now rejoice and give God praise for what He's done!

Some of you are in the hospital. Get up out of that bed that you're lying in. In the name of Jesus, I say unto you, Arise! Arise and be healed! Be delivered and be set free. The devil is a liar. Don't listen to him. You're going to rise and be healed! Go ahead! Do something you haven't done before. Let the devil know you're not putting up with his sickness anymore. You're healed! You're healed! You're healed!

FINANCIAL
MIRACLES

INTRODUCTION
"THE MIRACLE OF GIVING"

"Give, and it will be given to you: good measure, pressed down, shaken together, and running over will be put into your bosom. For with the same measure that you use, it will be measured back to you." *(Luke 6:38)*

Throughout the years I have learned an important truth — giving is a powerful tool for the miraculous.

God loves giving. It moves His heart. When we give, it is an expression of our total trust and obedience to God. Doors are opened in the supernatural realm when we give to God.

God wants to bless His people. He loves to pour out showers of blessing on those who serve him. The testimonies that you are about to read will attest to that fact. Through these people's stories, you will see what the Lord can do through people that give to Him.

But listen to me. If we want the blessing of God in our lives, we must learn this principle — the blessing follows obedience.

"Will a man rob God? Yet you have robbed Me! But you say, 'In what way have we robbed You?' In tithes and offerings. You are cursed with a curse, For you have robbed Me, Even this whole nation. Bring all the tithes into the storehouse, That there may be food in My house, And try Me now in this," Says the Lord of hosts, "If I will not open for you the windows of heaven and pour out for you such blessing that there will not be room enough to receive it." (Malachi 3:8-10)

Just imagine that. God wants to pour out a blessing on His people that's too big for them to receive!

But blessing only comes when we commit ourselves to obeying God by giving to Him. You cannot disobey God in the area of tithing without locking God's blessing out of your life. If you are a Christian, you should be going to the house of God weekly to worship and you should pay your tithes there.

Too many individuals 'worship' all week at the shopping mall shrines and pay more than tithes there. Then, when they come to the house of God they have nothing left to give. No wonder God's people are bound up with debt and financial difficulty.

You might say, "Brother Schambach, I would love give to God, but I just don't have anything to give. I don't have any money."

Good! Since you don't have anything, you won't be able to take credit for it when God performs a miracle. He will get all the glory! God usually sends me to people who don't have anything. I have seen countless times how God has provided when there was a need, all because somebody stepped out in faith and planted a seed.

Listen, it's a Biblical principle that when you step out in faith and plant, God will see to it that you reap a blessing. A little widow woman in the inner city taught me this lesson.

When I was pastoring a church in Newark, a dear lady, Mother Valez, came to me and said, "God told me to give my rent money in the offering."

I asked her, "Mother, when is your rent due?"

"In three days," she said.

I didn't want to take her rent money. No way! I was her pastor, and I didn't want to see her in financial difficulty. I rolled that money back into her hand and told her to pay her rent.

I'll never forget what she said to me.

"Are you trying to cheat me out of my blessing? You didn't ask for it, God did! Now take it."

She hit me where it hurt. So I took her offering, humbled by her response. That woman taught me something.

Later on that week Mother Valez came to church with another offering. Not only did God pay the rent, but she had even more to give back to Him.

That wasn't the best part of her testimony, though. She and I had been praying for her sons to be saved.

She said, "Brother Schambach, those two boys you and I have been praying and fasting for got saved this morning!"

This story blesses me so much because it illustrates the point that God blesses those who give.

I told that story in Haiti, which is one of the poorest nations in our hemisphere. You see, the Bible I preach works everywhere in the world just like it works here in the United States. If it doesn't work *everywhere*, then it's not true *anywhere*!

I told the story of Mother Valez to those people in Haiti, and the next night a little woman came to me with an offering. Seventy thousand people were there for that service, and I wanted all of them to hear what this little lady had to say.

She said, "Remember that story Pastor told last night? Well, if God can do it in there, He can do it here in Haiti. My rent is due tomorrow. I don't have enough to pay it, so I'm just going to give God everything I have. They won't take it anyway. I'm going to trust God to do it!"

All the Haitian preachers on that platform were sitting there saying, "Oh, Lord. This isn't Newark. This is Port-au-Prince."

All of a sudden, I saw a man coming from the middle of that crowd. He said, "God spoke to me. He told me to pay that woman's rent for three months. Here's the check for it."

Hallelujah! God always has a miracle waiting for us if we'll just step out in faith and do what He's calling us to do. He will bless us beyond measure, not just financially, but in every other way, too.

Be encouraged. Your back may be up against the wall right now financially. You're about to read some more stories of people who had their backs against the wall, but they stepped out in faith, believing that God would provide. As you read their testimonies, let faith stir in your heart, and know that God wants to do the same thing for you.

26
OBEDIENCE PAYS OFF

Many years ago, I bought a theater in Brooklyn, New York. Back then, I couldn't get churches to sponsor my meetings. I was too radical. We got so many people saved, I had to buy my own building and start a church, because I surely couldn't send them to those cold, dead churches.

So I went there to raise money for the thing. If I stayed ten days, surely I could get the down payment for the building.

There was a man who desperately needed a new truck. He was driving an old piece of junk. Have you ever driven one of those things? You've got to lay hands on it before it starts, then you have to lay hands on it to make it stop!

The first night, this man came walking down the aisle. He said, "Brother Schambach, God spoke to me."

I said, "What did God tell you to do, brother?"

"Well, I've been saving for a new truck," he said. "But every time I save, another emergency comes, and I've got to dip into that fund. Now, I have some money here that I've been saving for that truck. While you were praying, the Lord spoke to me."

"Tell me what He said, brother," I pleaded.

"Well, I've got $500 in my pocket," he said. "And God told me if I gave him that $500, He'll give me a new truck."

I said, "Who told you that?"

"God did," he replied.

"Well get your money out! You can't buy a new truck anywhere for $500. If God said He'll do it, He's going to do it!"

First of all, God wants you to be obedient. I want to encourage you in your own finances that God wants to bless you — everything that your hands touch. But you've got to be obedient to the word of the Lord.

So that man turned the money loose.

The next night he came in there with an envelope that was so big it could have choked an elephant! I mean, it was huge. That's because there were twenty-six $100 bills inside.

"Oh, brother," I said, "there must be a story here!"

So I gave him the microphone and he told us one of the craziest stories I've ever heard in my life!

He was driving that old wreck of a truck down the streets of Brooklyn, and God spoke to him and said, "Stop the truck! Get out of the truck and lift up the hood."

When he did, God said, "Look down by the carburetor."

Now, God wouldn't talk to me like that, because if He asked me to look for the carburetor, I'd open the trunk. I don't know where it is. I'm not mechanically inclined. But this man knew where it was.

So the man looked down under the carburetor. He said, "Am I losing my mind? I'm looking, and I don't see anything but a carburetor." So he shut the hood, got back in and started chugging back down the street. But God stopped him again.

"I told you to stop this truck and look down there by the carburetor."

So he stopped the truck and lifted the hood. He said, "Lord, I'm looking."

God said, "Look with your hand."

When he put his hand down by the carburetor, he got a hold of something that didn't belong there. It was a roll the size of an oil filter, all covered with grease. God said, "That's it. Break it off."

He broke it off. Inside that baked grease was $26,000, all in hundred dollar bills. He was able to buy a brand new truck, and had brought me the tithes from the money.

When he told his story, that whole church went wild. They started hollering, screaming and praising God. There were about a half a dozen men that got up and ran out. I think they were out there looking under their carburetors!

Praise God! This man gave an offering, and the Lord saw his heart.

When you're in financial need, you think maybe God is going to talk to somebody wealthy to come and give you help. Don't ever wonder how He is going to do it, because God's just going to turn around and do it some other way. He moves in mysterious ways!

27
BROTHER KEITH PROVES GOD

Read with me in *Mark 12:41-44*.

"Now Jesus sat opposite the treasury and saw how the people put money into the treasury. And many who were rich put in much. Then one poor widow came and threw in two mites, which make a quadrans. So He called His disciples to Himself and said to them, 'Assuredly, I say to you that this poor widow has put in more than all those who have given to the treasury; for they all put in out of their abundance, but she out of her poverty put in all that she had, her whole livelihood.'"

I love that story! Jesus said that this woman gave more than ALL of the other people who gave to the treasury.

That doesn't make any sense to the natural mind. It would seem that other people gave a lot more money than she did. But God does His own math! All those rich people had plenty to spare. But this precious little woman gave everything she had.

God wants us to lay it all on the line. That's what this woman did, and Jesus took notice.

A brother named Keith illustrated this principle.

I was holding a crusade in Baltimore. Keith and his wife came with some friends to the day service, where they heard my daughter, Donna, preach.

During the service, someone broke into the van they had ridden in. After this, they decided to just go home rather than staying for the evening service.

But then they ran into me. While they were waiting in the lobby of a nearby hotel for the police to arrive and take their report, we crossed paths. I greeted them like I would anybody else.

After we met, God told them to stay for the evening service and hear my message.

Now, Keith and his wife only had a few dollars between them. After paying the parking fee, they had $.35 each. They were embarrassed to put only $.35 in the offering plate, but it was all they had, so they gave it.

It wasn't only the offering that they were worried about, though. Keith and his wife were heavily invested in their own ministry at the time, a home for troubled girls. They had bills to pay, but didn't see how they were going to pay them. God knew. He saw their faith as they put the little they had in the offering.

Keith made a vow to God the next day. He said, "If you bless us with some money today, I'll give what I would like to have given last night. I'll give Brother Schambach $200."

That day, they received a check in the mail for $1,750!

It didn't matter to God that they had hardly any money. What mattered to Him was their faith. He honored that faith when they were obedient to Him.

28
WOMAN PLEDGES, GOD PROVIDES

Not long ago, the Lord placed it on my heart to challenge people to give to God in a special way. He instructed me to tell them to pledge $2,000, and to send the tithe on that, which is $200. The Lord told me that in 90 days, He would provide the other $1,800. After this step of faith, God would set them free from the bondage of debt, and bless them in their finances.

Well, a woman named Doria took me up on that challenge.

In April of 2000, she heard my message. She had been out of work for 6 months after being laid off from a high-paying "tech" job. She had house payments to make on her newly constructed home, which she had moved into two months before being laid off. But she continued to tithe to the Lord on her unemployment checks, and on her back vacation pay. She knew the Lord would provide.

When she heard my challenge to pledge the $2,000, she didn't have much to give. But that's when God gets the most glory!

Doria trusted God, and pledged the entire $2,000, which she intended to pay on with her federal income tax return. In addition to this, she pledged to support the ministry monthly.

The following month, in May, her back vacation pay ran out. Now she was dependent on her unemployment checks, which were only about 1/4 of her former income. But God saw her through these rough times. June came, and still nothing happened.

Then, in early July (exactly 90 days after she pledged the money) she was contacted by a recruiter who told her a Fortune 500 company wanted to hire her. God had provided!

Her new job paid $90,000 a year. She also received a sign-on bonus of $2,500 (God provided for the faith promise) and a relocation check for $10,000. To top it all off, this new job had an even better benefit package than the company for which she had previously worked.

She was faithful to God, and God was faithful to her. She ended up with more than she started with!

Listen, dear friend. I have seen God do extraordinary things when His people respond to Him in faith. Yet, I've also had situations in which people responded to a challenge God has given, and they did not receive the results they desired.

Perhaps there is a secret there — we must not give with our primary focus on being what God will do for us. We give, partnering with His purposes, generously contributing toward His mission.

God is excited when His children have generous spirits and trust Him. He never leaves His children in lack.

"Now to Him who is able to do exceedingly abundantly above all that we ask or think, according to the power that works in us, to Him be glory in the church by Christ Jesus to all generations, forever and ever. Amen." (Ephesians 3:20-21)

29
THE WOMAN WHO ALMOST FORGOT

Sharon had never been to one of my meetings before. Loved ones had tried to get her into revival services for years, but she wouldn't go. She was saved, but had no interest in crusades, or "revivals", as we call them. She didn't know what she was missing.

Finally, when I had a tent crusade in Newark in 1998, Sharon decided to come. She also brought a friend. That night I was talking about the $2,000 pledge. I challenged the people like God had instructed me to do. I told them to sow their seed.

So Sharon and her friend agreed to pledge the money. She sowed what she had, but then forgot about it.

Shortly thereafter, Sharon was hired to a new job. Now, she hadn't asked God for a new job, but He gave her one anyway. She got a $5,000 increase doing the same work that she had done before. Still, she didn't remember the pledge. Her friend received a $3,000 increase in her job. Still, she didn't remember the pledge.

Her friend had to remind her of the faith promise they had made. Well, God blesses us even if we don't know He's doing it.

That wasn't all God did for Sharon. Over the course of the next two years, she received a total salary increase of $12,000. Also, she needed a new home, because she had to move out of her old one. So she cried out to the Lord, "Where do I go? What do I do?"

The Lord led her to a certain house. She didn't have the money for a down payment, but she went anyway. When she applied, they told her they would have to run her credit.

"Oh, no!" she thought. "I can forget it."

But when they ran her credit, it came back clean. God had performed a miracle.

The last time I saw Sharon, she was in the process of purchasing that home, and was shouting and giving God praise for what He had done. Thank the Lord, when we make a covenant with Him, He is faithful to keep His promises. He never forgets.

30
THE $78,000 MIRACLE

When I was in Lexington, Kentucky, I met some other folks who took me up on that same challenge. It was a husband and wife - Curtis and Mary Lou.

Both of them had grown up in a religious church, but they had not heard much faith teaching.

Well, the Lord started to lead them in new ways. As they started watching Christian television programming, God began building their faith.

They saw this old preacher proclaiming God's Word, demonstrating the Gospel of Christ. They told me later that I was instrumental in building their faith.

Now, like I've been telling you, I believe in planting seeds and expecting to reap a harvest. That's how God's financial system works. Curtis and Mary Lou learned about this as they watched their television. But as they watched, something I said scared them to death.

"Listen to what the man of God says. I want you to sow a $2,000 seed."

The reason this scared them was that they had made some bad financial decisions. They hadn't been walking in all the things that they believed. Also, they just were not familiar with the concept of sowing financial seeds and reaping a harvest.

This was a wake-up call for them. Yet, they didn't have the funds to make that kind of a pledge.

Now, when I challenge people like this, I know they don't have it. I'm trying to teach them how to trust in God.

This couple heard me talking about the pledge to be debt-free by sowing a seed, and even though they didn't have it, they took the challenge. They made a vow to God that they would send in any money that was above what they normally made. Then they made out a list of all the debt that they owed, believing for God to cancel them.

Over the next 90 days, the devil was after them. He didn't want them to get blessed, so he tried to choke off any extra money they received.

They were renting a building to a lady who decided to move out during the first month after their pledge. That was November.

They had also been receiving rent money from a man that was staying with them. In December, the second month after their pledge, he moved out. That cost them more money.

In January, to top it all off the transmission in their car went out!

They were really being tested! But they were determined to trust God and honor their promise to Him. They weren't going to let the devil defeat them.

By the end of the 90 days, they had managed to pay the entire $2,000 pledge off. And then came the best part.

At the time, Mary Lou had an appeal with the government. It had been pending since 1992. The government owed them some money. It was their faith that triggered the blessing.

In a short time, that appeal went through, and they received a check in the mail for $63,000 — from the U.S. government! Now that is a miracle!

As if that wasn't enough, there is even more to their story.

When Mary Lou found out that I was bringing my tent to Lexington in 2001, she made another pledge. That area had never received this kind of ministry before, and she wanted to help bring it to pass. So she pledged to send me $1,000.

She didn't have that sum, but she sent what she had — only $10 — trusting that God would provide the rest.

Well, just a few days before my crusade started, she received another letter in the mail from the government. They said that they had made a mistake, and that they actually owed her and her husband more money – over $15,000 more!

Hallelujah! God provided the rest of the pledge and more. Oh, this just blesses me to see this outstanding miracle. When my tent crusade started there in Lexington, this precious couple came up to the platform to testify. You should have heard the shouting that went on in that tent when they told their story!

I get so thrilled when God honors the faith of His children, especially those who are just learning. Although they were a little frightened, they moved in faith, and God honored that faith.

Sometimes God will ask you to give something that seems impossible to give. Don't hold back. When He speaks, you can trust His promises.

31
THE ANGEL AND THE REAL ESTATE

One of the greatest testimonies, I believe, that I have heard regarding the $2,000 challenge was given by a dear elderly woman in one of my meetings. She put God to the test, and He proved faithful.

This woman was watching my telecast and heard me talking about the faith promise. She sat there and thought to herself, "I'm going to put God to the test."

That's what I tell people to do. Put Him to the test!

So she wrote a check out for $200, the tithe on the pledge. She addressed it, put a stamp on it, and laid it on the coffee table. The next morning, she took it to the post office.

When she returned home, before she could set her purse down, there was a knock at the door. She didn't see anybody pull in behind her. Nobody had followed her in. But suddenly there was this knock at the door.

She opened the door, and there was a man standing there. "I want to buy some land," he said.

Now this dear lady owned eight acres of land. She had tried to sell it. She went to nearly every realtor in town. They all told her it wouldn't sell because there were three high-powered gas lines through it. They told her the land couldn't be used for anything.

She told the visitor, "I've got some. But I don't guess you'll want it." She told him the truth about the land – why she couldn't sell it – but he wanted to see it anyway.

So she took him out there to see it. To her amazement, he said, "I'll tell you what. I'll give you a hundred thousand dollars for it."

Wow! What a miracle! On the very same day, God provided because she was obedient to what the man of God told her to do.

You see, that's what I mean. When you hear the man or woman of God say something you wonder, "Are they just talking?" But when you step out in faith, you're not just being obedient to what a person says, you are being obedient to what God Himself says, speaking through the channel of a preacher.

When she testified under the tent, she told me that the weeds have grown on that property, and nobody has seen that man since. I believe it was an angel of the Lord!

32
DON'T EAT YOUR SEED

I want to talk to you pastors out there. Listen to me, God wants to bless you, too.

I have seen God pull churches out of debt. I've seen it here in America, in Europe, in Canada — all over the world. Everywhere I go I preach about the blessing that comes from giving to God.

I want all of you that are in the ministry to pay close attention to this story.

There was a woman named Sharon who was pastoring a church with her husband in Bellis, Alberta. One night they were watching television and saw me preach a sermon on the miracle of giving.

They were in a desperate situation. If they didn't have $40,000 very soon, their church was going to be shut down. But when they heard the message, faith came alive in their heart.

They phoned the television station and pledged to give to God. Now, they didn't have the money, but they believed that God would provide.

Two days later, they received $1,000 from an unexpected source.

Now they needed this money desperately. But they had made a promise to give to the Lord, to plant a seed.

Listen, folks, you can't eat your seed! Don't worry, God can provide $40,000 just as easily as he can provide $1,000. If you do what He tells you to do, He will take care of you.

So even though they needed that $1,000, they sent it in.

Fourteen days later, a $40,000 check was put in their hands!

Hear me, pastors. It works! They were at the bottom. They didn't have anything. But they stood on God's Word and planted a seed, and then reaped a great harvest.

Is your church in financial trouble? Then exercise your faith and plant a seed. I'm telling you, when you give to God, He's going to meet the need. You cannot out-give God.

33
GOD'S BUSINESS

Our ministry has what we call Power Partners. They not only pray with me, but they help the ministry financially every month, and God blesses them because of it.

Mary Cavicchi is a faithful partner of mine. She owns a rehabilitation company in Wisconsin. God worked a mighty miracle for her business because she gave sacrificially to Him.

Now, she was no stranger to the miracle-working power of God. She had already seen first-hand what God can do for those who have faith in Him.

In the summer of 1998, she fractured her knee so badly that the doctor told her she would need a total knee replacement. It was around this time that she had been introduced to my ministry.

She listened to a series of my audiotapes in her car. As she listened to those tapes, she let her faith build and build. She found out that I was going to be holding a crusade in her area. So she told her surgeon to wait until after she went to the crusade.

To make a long story short, Jesus healed her knee. She still has the X-rays to prove it!

Months later, in October of 1998, she was on a business trip in Arlington, Texas, when two men attacked her in her hotel room. They robbed her and beat her to a pulp. She woke up in the emergency room.

The doctor told her she had a closed head injury, double vision, and that she was badly beaten all over. She wasn't even able to sit on the edge of her bed without falling over. But she was confident that the Lord would heal her.

The normal human reaction would be to hate those men who could do such a thing. But that wasn't Mary's reaction. She forgave them. She prayed for them to get saved.

It was her forgiveness that unlocked the power of God in her life. The next day the double vision was gone. Two days later she could stand. Three days later she could walk. Four days later she was released to go home. God restored her health.

So as you can see, Mary had seen the power of God in action. But we're talking about financial miracles. Well, God did that, too!

Mary's company was the seventh largest woman-owned company in Wisconsin in 1998. But 1999 was a rough year.

They lost a great deal of money in the first 6 months. They were in a financial tailspin! So do you know what Mary did? She got on her face and cried out to God. She just committed the situation to Him.

The Lord reminded her of when she had been attacked by those men. "Mary, just as I sustained you, I will sustain the company."

Mary had already been tithing to Schambach Ministries out of what her company made. But during this time, she promised God that she would start double tithing if He would see them through the year. Well, 85% of the rehab companies in the United States went out of business, but the Lord allowed her company to break even.

You may say, "Well, that's not much of a miracle." Just wait. The best part is yet to come!

In January of 2000, the company made more money than it had in the entire 22 ½ years that it had been in existence! In just one month!

Hallelujah! God blessed Mary because she made her business His business.

34
COW MONEY

Years ago in Seattle, two tornadoes tore through and destroyed our tent. Now, it was the devil that caused this disaster. But God can take a disaster, turn it around, and work it for His glory.

We could not continue services in the tent, so I looked for a building. The Civic Auditorium was available over the next seventeen days. We didn't miss a meeting. And before we left town, enough money came in to buy a brand new tent.

The devil just doesn't have any sense. The old tent that he destroyed was full of holes anyway. Now we had a brand new one!

But it was a 12-year-old boy that started the whole thing off.

I received the offering one night, and I happened to see a little boy walking down the aisle with a $5 bill in his hand. Tears were running down his face. You know how we human beings often make snap judgments and form first impressions. I thought, *"I wonder what that kid is crying for? His mama gave him that five dollars. Maybe he just didn't want to walk down here with it."*

He headed right for the bucket that I was holding. I said, "What are you crying for, boy?"

He threw the five dollars in the bucket and said, "Brother Schambach, that's my cow in there!"

I looked in the bucket and said, "Your what?"

I knew I had a story there, so I put the bucket in one of the pastor's hands. I took the little boy aside and said, "Tell me about it."

"I always wanted a cow of my own," he said. "But we lived in the city limits, and there's an ordinance that says you can't have a cow in the backyard. But nine months ago, Dad moved out into the country. He called me and said I could have a cow now - but I had to pay for it. For nine months I've been saving my dimes. I've been running errands. I picked up a paper route. I get up at four in the morning and deliver newspapers. I've been saving five dollars for nine months."

I said, "Why are you putting that cow money in?"

He said, "I heard God's voice."

My God, that's the miracle to me! Giving five dollars is no miracle. But can you imagine getting a 12-year-old boy to hear the voice of God? I asked, "How did you know it was God?"

He said, "He called me by my name. He said if I gave the cow money, He would give me the cow."

I looked at him and said, "Are you sure God told you that?"

"Yes, sir. He told me that."

I said, "Then dry up those tears! You're getting the best end of the deal!"

While the other folks were bringing their offerings, I sort of held onto his shoulder. I told all those people in that Civic Auditorium what I just told you about that boy.

Then a big 6'7", 270-pound man in bib overalls got up. He started crying. He walked up, and I said, "What are you crying for, brother?"

He said, "God just spoke to me."

I said, "What did God tell you?"

He said, "He told me to give that boy a cow."

I looked up and down at him. I learned this lesson a long time ago: the folks with the fancy suits don't have the money. It's the guys wearing the overalls. The guys with the suits on have all their money in the suits!

So I kind of did a double take on him and said, "Brother, do you have a cow?"

"I've got thousands of them, Brother Schambach," he replied. He was the biggest rancher in the state of Washington. When God told that boy to give, He already had a cow waiting!

The following Saturday this rancher had a Polaroid picture shot of the boy with his cow. He said to me, "Brother Schambach, I wish you could have been out at the ranch today. That boy came out with his daddy in a rented trailer to pick up his cow. I told him to go pick out any one he wanted. You know, that rascal picked the best one I had! And he never even thanked me for it. He just put his arm around that cow and raised the other arm up and said, 'Thank you, Jesus, for my cow!'"

He knew exactly Who to thank — the cattle on a thousand hills belong to God! (*Psalm 50:10*) God surely knows how to speak to a rancher to turn one of them loose.

After that little boy told his story, you should have seen how much money came in that offering. You don't have to beg people to give. You show them how God blesses and they'll want to get in on that blessing.

God was teaching that boy a principle, and teaching me a principle through that boy.

35
NO SENSE, JUST FAITH

I'll never forget the first church building I bought. It was an old Jewish YWHA in New Jersey. I rented it for three months, preached in it, and so many folks got saved in it, I thought I might as well just buy the building and establish a church. But there was no way to do it — I didn't even have a bank account.

One day, while we were still renting, I was studying my message. I was going to preach on *Deuteronomy 11:24,* which says, *"Every place on which the sole of your foot treads shall be yours."* Oh, Lord! I knew I wasn't just preaching to those people, I was preaching to myself.

I laid hands on about 500 people that night, but I couldn't wait to close that service. After it was over, I got my Bible, went out, and I said to some of my preacher friends, "Come with me. We're going to walk around the building and lay some footprints down. I'm going to claim this thing."

I couldn't buy it. I had never had a bank account. I had never written a check. I didn't have any sense, but I had faith.

When I told my preacher friends that I was going to walk around that building and claim it, they said, "We'll wait in the car. You go ahead and walk."

I've learned this: When you put your faith to work, sometimes you have to do it all by yourself. God said every bit of ground that the soles of *your* feet tread on, you shall possess it.

I walked around that building, and the next day they put a "For Sale" sign on the lawn. I pulled it out, marched down to the realtor's office and asked him, "Who put this on my property?" He thought I was crazy, since he knew I had been renting the place.

He said, "What do you want to offer me for that building?"

I said, "Nothing."

"Well," he said, "Come back when you have money."

I said, "Now hold on here a minute. I believe in starting low."

He said, "We just had an offer of $265,000. An insurance company owns it, and I know they won't sell for less than that."

Just then the Holy Ghost said, "Offer them $75,000." Now, if He had told me to offer $1 million, I would have done it, because I didn't have a dime anyway. There's no difference between $75,000 and a $1 million if you don't have anything at all. Zero is zero. That's why it's always good to obey God. You don't have to be afraid of anything. You started with nothing, you're going to end with nothing.

I said, "I'll give you $75,000."

He didn't want to do it, but when I insisted, he picked up the phone and called the chairman of the board of this insurance company. Turning away from me, I could hear him say, "I have a crazy preacher in my office. I told him you folks turned down an offer of $265,000, but he told me to offer you $75,000. I told him there's no way you'll do it. And...what did you say? Would you say that one more time? Well, all right. It's your building. Yes, sir."

He hung up the phone and turned around to me. "He told me to sell it to you for $75,000."

I said, "What happened?"

Dumbfounded, that realtor explained, "The board of directors were meeting when I called. They had such a great year in life insurance that they said to give it to the preacher for $75,000, and they would take a loss on the taxes. You're not so dumb after all, are you, preacher?"

I said, "No, sir."

He said, "Now, how much money do you have for a down payment?"

I said, "Nothing."

He asked for $35,000 down. God provided $25,000. The night before I had to come up with the money, we were still $10,000 short, and I didn't know what we'd do. A local preacher asked me, "What are you going to do?"

I said, "Nothing. I didn't do anything when I first started; I'm not going to do anything now. There's no time to worry now. There's no way God's going to let the devil whip Him in a business deal. God's the best businessman I've ever seen. He always finishes what He starts."

I sat in that office the next day and waited until ten minutes before noon. Noon was the deadline! Then a little woman came walking up. I ran out to her and said, "Give it to me! Give it to me!"

She said, "How do you know I have something for you?"

I said, "I'll talk to you later; just turn it loose and give it to me. It's got to be you. God's never cut it so close!" She reached into her purse and took out a $10,000 cashier's check. I grabbed that thing and went down to the bank. The building belonged to me!

After it was over, one of those preachers who wouldn't march around the building with me in the first place called me on the phone from Englewood and said, "I found a building here in Englewood that I want for a church. Come on over and walk around it for me."

I said, "Well, I'm about twenty-eight minutes from you, but I'll make it in twenty. Wait for me. But remember, brother, if I use my feet, it's going to be my building!"

He never even bothered to hang up — just left the phone dangling and ran over to that building. He didn't just march around it, he raced around it and laid down his size ten tracks. Guess what? God gave him his building!

God has a specific inheritance for you! Learn how to trust Him, and He'll lead you right to it!

I didn't have a lick of sense. I just had faith. And God brought me through. I do have one regret, though — I wish I would have walked around the whole block!

CONCLUSION
"STEP OUT ON THE WATER"

It works! It works! You can trust God to meet your need.

Now, anybody can trust Him when the checkbook is filled. But it takes faith to trust Him when the balance says 'double zero'. There's one thing that I've learned about God, though — He will make a way where there is no way.

If you are struggling in your finances, God wants to set you free. You do not have to be in bondage to debt or want. God wants you blessed. But you've got to step out on the water! You've got to let Him know that you mean business.

"But this I say: He who sows sparingly will also reap sparingly, and he who sows bountifully will also reap bountifully. So let each one give as he purposes in his heart, not grudgingly or of necessity; for God loves a cheerful giver. And God is able to make all grace abound toward you, that you, always having all sufficiency in all things, may have an abundance for every good work." (2 Corinthians 9:6-8)

When you allow giving to be a way of life for you, it becomes a miracle tool in your hand.

Allow God to develop a giving heart in you. It may be hard at first, but God can help you to be a cheerful giver. Remember, you are not giving to man, who can sometimes be unthankful or careless. You are giving to God.

But now I want to pray for you. If you're struggling financially, agree with me now, and believe God to perform a miracle.

Father, I come to You in the name Jesus. I bring this one before You whose back is against the wall. I come against the bondage of debt in their lives. Satan, you have got no business in their pocketbook, so I command you right now to loose your hold on their finances. Lord, I pray that You develop in this individual a giving heart. And Lord, as they learn to give to You, I pray that You would open up the windows of heaven and pour out a blessing on them. Let it be above what they could even ask or think. Give them a testimony that will bring glory to You alone. In Jesus' name I pray. Amen and amen.

MIRACLES ON FOREIGN SOIL

36.
ALL THE WORLD

"And He said to them, "Go into all the world and preach the gospel to every creature." (Mark 16:15)

I want you to know that we preach this message around the world — the saving, healing power of Christ. I have been to India, Russia, Bulgaria, Mexico, Brazil, Haiti, Indonesia — and many, many other places with this gospel of power. As I mentioned earlier, if it doesn't work everywhere, then it's not true. It has to work in other countries just like it works here in the United States. And let me tell you, it does! We see more miracles in foreign countries than we do here in the United States.

I remember going to Mexico City with T.L. Osborn, preaching to 60,000 people. I'll never forget praying just one prayer. Instantly, blind eyes were opened. Deaf ears came unstopped. No human hands were ever laid on them! Just one prayer! People were picking up their wheelchairs, holding them over their head and walking up to the platform to give God praise!

Let me tell you, what God has done in other countries through this ministry will absolutely blow your mind!

HAITI

I conducted a revival crusade in a stadium in Port-au-Prince, Haiti one year. On opening night, there were 35,000 people in that stadium. That night, I prayed a prayer for the people and left.

While I was going out, this little 12-year-old boy wrapped his hands around my leg and would not turn loose. While I was dragging him, he was saying something in Creole. I couldn't understand him, so I asked, "What in the world is he saying?"

My driver said, "I'll interpret for you. This boy is telling you he was born blind. When you prayed that one prayer, the lights came on. He can see!"

I picked that boy up and put him in the arms of one of the preachers and said, "Take him up there and let him tell the story." When we were driving out, it sounded like somebody had made a touchdown in there! The people had heard the boy's testimony.

Now, everybody in Port-au-Prince knew that boy. He had begged on the streets, and everyone knew he was totally blind. The news of his miracle spread, and the next night you couldn't get near the stadium. It was jam-packed with about 70,000 people, and many more outside who couldn't get in.

That triggered many more miracles throughout the entire crusade.

THE CARRIBEAN

By now you should know that I am so thankful for the means of radio to preach the gospel. It has been a tried and true method of reaching people all across this nation. Well, it's not different anywhere else. Thousands of people in foreign nations have been blessed by our broadcasts all over the world.

In the 1970's, my old church, Philadelphia Miracle Temple, was sponsoring my radio broadcasts in the Caribbean. I knew these people needed the gospel, too. Yet, I wasn't sure if we were really reaching them.

So I decided to conduct a long crusade throughout the Caribbean. I wanted to see if the investment Philadelphia Miracle Temple was making was really touching lives. This crusade went from the Virgin Islands to St. Kitts, St. Vincent, Trinidad and the Port of Spain.

In St. Kitts, 35,000 people showed up for the first meeting — on an island with a population of just 50,000!

When I met the governor of St. Kitts, he told me, "The entire island comes to a halt when your radio broadcast airs each day." Wow!

There was a mighty demonstration of the power of God. During that meeting, 50 people jumped out of wheelchairs! And so many deaf ears were unstopped that the school for the deaf there in St. Kitts had to be shut down! Hallelujah!

Now, that crusade service was broadcast on live radio to the island of Antigua. It shook them up, too!

The next day a delegation from Antigua came and begged me to preach on their island. Of course, I hadn't planned to go there. My schedule was full as it was, and I only had two days of rest planned during the entire crusade. Now, I'm human. I get tired just like everybody else. I told them this, but they just wouldn't take 'no' for an answer.

"You can rest after the rapture!" they said. "We need you in Antigua now."

So I went, and God moved miraculously.

I never had to wonder again whether the Caribbean broadcasts were reaching people!

INDONESIA

I'm not ashamed to preach about the baptism of the Holy Ghost. A lot of preachers don't believe in this, or they are ashamed to speak it from the pulpit. Not me! I like to shout it from the rooftops. I like to splash it all over TV and radio. I like to let people know that God wants to fill them with the Holy Ghost and fire!

Read with me in *Acts 2:1-4*:

"When the Day of Pentecost had fully come, they were all with one accord in one place. And suddenly there came a sound from heaven, as of a rushing mighty wind, and it filled the whole house where they were sitting. Then there appeared to them divided tongues, as of fire, and one sat upon each of them. And they were all filled with the Holy Spirit and began to speak with other tongues, as the Spirit gave them utterance."

The record is very clear that the tongues of fire sat upon each of them, and they were all filled with the Holy Ghost. And when they were all filled with the Holy Ghost, they began to speak in tongues as the Spirit gave them utterance. Before the Day of Pentecost, there is no record that any person ever spoke an unlearned language as a result of the moving of God's Spirit.

In Acts 2, it talks of a *"rushing mighty wind," "tongues, as of fire,"* and says that they were speaking *"with other tongues."* Later in Acts 10, it says they were speaking with tongues and magnifying God. Finally, in Acts 19, it refers to speaking with tongues and prophecy.

In each instance, there was an additional manifestation, but only speaking with tongues occurred every time. You see, this was to be the initial evidence that believers had been filled with the Holy Ghost. It signified that the early church had received "the promise of the Father" and "the Comforter" that Jesus had promised.

Well, the Holy Ghost is just as real to us in this day as He was for the early church. I have experienced this many times, but one of the greatest examples I have seen came when I was preaching in Indonesia. 30,000 people gathered on a field to hear me preach.

Now, I was tired. I had been preaching all through that area. I had preached to so many people, and I was really tired in my body. When I was getting ready to preach that day, I prayed, "Oh, Lord. Please spare this old flesh of mine. Let Your Spirit come on everybody that's out in that field."

All of a sudden, 10,000 people fell out under the power of God. Like a breath of wind! I looked in front of me, and 10,000 more people fell out. Then I looked to the side, and the last 10,000 people fell out. Right there in front of me! No catchers. They were all fallers, and they all fell out right on the field.

There I was, standing all by myself. So I looked around at my interpreter, and he was out! I said, "Lord, I feel like I've been left out. Knock me out, too."

God said, "Walk through the crowd of the people."

So I walked out there. Toward the back, there was a group of young people, Indonesian young people. They were speaking in English. In English! It blew my mind.

I ran up and got my interpreter off the ground. I said, "Get up quick!"

"What?" he replied. "What do you want me to do?"

I said, "Come with me. I want you to see and hear what I found."

So he came back with me and showed him.

"You got me up out of the Spirit for this?" he said. "Oh, Brother Schambach, that's a common occurrence. They're receiving the Holy Ghost. They don't know English, but this is a sign to them that they received the baptism of the Holy Ghost."

You see, I know English. It's not an unknown tongue to me. It wasn't to my interpreter either. He knew English as well as his native language. But these young people didn't know English. Nobody had ever taught them this. It was the utterance of the Holy Spirit. That was the initial evidence to them.

You might be wondering about the baptism of the Holy Ghost. Your pastor might tell you that it's not for today, or that it's not for everyone today, just some. Well, I'm telling you it's for you.

God has provided a mighty in-filling of the Holy Ghost and power to carry His people over the turbulent times of these last days. You need this! It is for you! Let God baptize you in the Holy Ghost and fire!

SEMARANGH, INDONESIA

There was another miracle that took place in Indonesia that blew my mind. I cannot explain how it happened. All I know is that it happened!

I was conducting meetings in Semarang. On the opening night, there was a torrential downpour. I mean, everything was drenched. (I really know when to have an outdoor meeting!) But the place was still packed out. Not one of those people moved. They stood there and listened to me preach.

Some of my associates wanted to give me an umbrella to put over me, but I said, "No. If they're going to stand in the rain to hear me, I'm going to preach to them in the rain."

So I preached to them in the rain! And God did so many great miracles that day. I laid hands on people. Blind eyes were opened. Deaf ears were unstopped. Cripples were walking. It was powerful!

Because of the large crowd, there were army guards all around. They'd never had crowds of that capacity before. One of these soldiers, who was a colonel in the army and a Muslim, came to me and said, "Would you pray for me?"

"What's wrong with you?" I said.

"Well, I got shot in this eye. The bullet is still in there, and I can't see out of that eye."

Now, I knew this man was a Muslim. So I made it clear to him what name I pray in – the name of Jesus. He is the only miracle-worker. Mohammed can't hear me pray because he is still in the grave. But Jesus is alive! Hallelujah!

"I pray in the name of Jesus," I told him.

"Use any name you want," he replied. "I've seen too much here!"

So I prayed for that colonel in the name of Jesus. I can't explain what happened after that. It is hard to fathom! I am not a chemist. I'm not a scientist. But after I put my hand on that eye and asked God to perform a miracle, the bullet melted right into my hand, and God restored perfect vision to the eye.

That man got saved and filled with the Spirit, and God called him to preach.

Now, he would have been up for retirement in six months, but he went immediately and resigned his commission! He said, "I want to travel all over Indonesia and tell my people that Jesus is Lord!"

Listen to me. He wasn't saved when God performed the miracle. He was still a sinner. Many Christians don't like to hear that. But God did it anyway, and it was that miracle that opened his eyes to the gospel, and to the power of Jesus Christ. Now he's shaking up Indonesia!

SURIBIA, INDONESIA

There was another Muslim man that came to me for a miracle. But this one was not a soldier. He was a priest.

He brought his wife to me, who was demon-possessed. Doctors couldn't help her. His religion couldn't help her. She was bound by the devil.

So he brought her to me for prayer. Then when I laid hands on her, the strangest thing happened. All of a sudden, there were thumbtacks and nails coming out of her skin. I've never seen anything like it before. It blew me away! God delivered her and set her free.

The next night the man came back to the service. While I was receiving the offering, he came up to the front and threw something in the bucket. It was wrapped up in a newspaper, and was so heavy that the bucket fell out of my hand.

I grabbed him by the shoulder and pulled him back. I said, "What in the world do you got in there?"

"Look," he said.

I opened it up and discovered that it was a brick of solid gold!

Then he told his story: "I've had my wife everywhere. Doctors couldn't do anything. My religion couldn't do anything. I brought her here and you laid hands on her in the name of Jesus, and she was delivered. I answered that altar call, and now I'm a Jesus man. And I wanted to bring you that offering."

I gave the gold to our missionary there, and told him to build a new home for orphans.

EPILOGUE
"FAITH THAT GOES THE DISTANCE"

"Then Jesus went out from there and departed to the region of Tyre and Sidon. And behold, a woman of Canaan came from that region and cried out to Him, saying, 'Have mercy on me, O Lord, Son of David! My daughter is severely demon-possessed.' But He answered her not a word. And His disciples came and urged Him, saying, 'Send her away, for she cries out after us.' But He answered and said, 'I was not sent except to the lost sheep of the house of Israel.' Then she came and worshipped Him, saying, 'Lord, help me!' But He answered and said, 'It is not good to take the children's bread and throw it to the little dogs.' And she said, 'Yes, Lord, yet even the little dogs eat the crumbs which fall from their masters' table.' Then Jesus answered and said to her, 'O woman, great is your faith! Let it be to you as you desire.' And her daughter was healed from that very hour." (Matthew 15:21-28)

This woman came to Jesus with a need. When she looked into His eyes, she saw a delivering power greater than any need she had.

It seemed at first that Jesus was putting her off, but He was not. He was simply telling the truth.

His mission was to preach salvation to the Jews. According to His call and mission, there was no way He could give this woman a miracle. But her faith caused her to press in and receive a miracle anyway! She would not take 'no' for an answer — even from Jesus. That's some kind of faith!

Friend, if you are a child of God, you don't have to beg like this woman did. You have been washed in the Blood of the Lamb. There is a table of God's goodness set out for you. All the power, anointing, gifts and fruits of God's Spirit belong to you. Partake of them. Enjoy them. Let God know you appreciate what He has prepared for you. Hallelujah!

Jesus, in response to this woman's refusal to be denied, said something He never said to Peter, James or John. He said, *"O woman, great is your faith; Let it be to you as you desire."* In today's language, that means, "Whatever you want, you've got it!"

And this brings up a point worth looking at: He didn't say, "What My will is, let that happen to you." He said, "Let it be to you as YOU desire."

Let me get really personal here for a moment, friend. What do you want from the Lord today? I hear people say, "Well, anything He wants to give me." But you see, that isn't the way faith works. He wants to know exactly what you want.

Perhaps you have loved ones who are facing great needs today. I want to encourage you again that you can stand in their place before Jesus and plead their cause. This is what intercession is all about.

Maybe it's you that has the need. I don't care whether it's for healing, deliverance, financial freedom — whatever it is, God wants to do it for you.

I trust that your faith has come alive as you have read these wonderful testimonies of God's miracle-working power. I'm here to tell you that what He did for these people, He'll do for you. You see, God is no respecter of persons. If He does something for one person, He's got to do it for everybody.

Psalm 34:19 says, *"Many are the afflictions of the righteous, But the Lord delivers him out of them all."* Not half of them. Not most of them. Not even 99.9% of them! The Bible says ALL of them!

You say, "Well, I've prayed and nothing happens." Well, keep on praying! Keep on asking! Don't give up. It's not over 'til it's over! You are coming out of this situation. You are going to be more than a conqueror. Hallelujah!

Press your way through. You don't know how close you are to your miracle! All you've got to do is keep on exercising your faith. God will do the rest. He has a miracle with your name written all over it!

Remember, the Bible says *everyone* that asks receives. That's you! That's me! That's everybody!

So get ready. Put your faith in God, and you will be in a position to receive the greatest miracle that you have ever experienced.

Miracles II: "Greater Miracles"